"There are few people who have impacted I more than Pastors Casey and Wendy innovation, and unrestrained belief in the potential of others has made me a better leader, and their friendship and loyalty over many years have made us better people. Casey and Wendy's personal stories are a testimony to the life changing power of Jesus Christ and the grace and kindness He extends to us all when we are born again. Their longevity in ministry and ability to adapt to the changing seasons of life and leadership is the perfect foundation from which to teach about the power of a renewed mind."

Brian Houston, Global Founder and Senior Pastor of Hillsong Church

I consider Casey an authority on the teaching of renewing the mind. He has an amazing testimony, and I believe that you will be greatly encouraged by this book.

Joseph Prince, Senior Pastor of New Creation Church

I tell people everywhere—because it is entirely the truth—that next to the Bible, the book that has most influenced my Christian walk more than any other is *Renewing the Mind*. Reading it changed the whole trajectory of my life. Maybe God could have done it another way, but I honestly don't know if I would be doing what I am doing today had I not read Renewing the Mind in 1992. It just so totally, radically changed my life and gave me hope for the first time.

Christine Caine, A21 Founder

Renewing the Mind 2.0

Casey and Wendy Treat

Renewing The Mind 2.0: With God's Grace, You Can Change
Copyright © 2023 by Christian Faith Center

ISBN: 9798376025390
February 2023
Christian Faith Center

This book is designed to provide accurate and authoritative information with regard to the subject matter covered. This information is given with the understanding that neither the author nor publisher is engaged in rendering legal or professional advice. Since the details of your situation are fact-dependent, you should additionally seek the services of a competent professional

Scripture quotations, unless otherwise indicated, are taken from the New King James Version®. Copyright © 1982 by Thomas Nelson. Used by permission. All rights reserved.

Scripture quotation marked TPT is from The Passion Translation®. Copyright © 2017, 2018 by Passion & Fire Ministries, Inc. Used by permission. All rights reserved. ThePassionTranslation.com.

Printed in the United States of America
All rights reserved under International Copyright Law.
Contents and/or cover may not be reproduced in whole or part in any form without the expressed written consent of the Author.

Casey Treat Ministries
Christian Faith Center
PO Box 98600
Seattle, WA 98198

www.caseytreat.com
www.christianfaith.us

DEDICATION

Wendy and I dedicate this book to three men who have changed our lives.

Julius Young led me to Jesus in 1976. He was a black man from Washington, D.C., and a generation older than me, but he became my spiritual father and our best friend. He founded WDRC (Washington Drug Rehabilitation Center) and was the first elder in our church.

Dr. Fred Price ordained us into ministry in 1980. He was our pastor and mentor for living our faith in a practical church setting. Fred taught us to use our faith and believe bigger.

Dr. David Yongi Cho came to Christian Faith Center in the early 1990's. He opened our eyes to visions and dreams that grew our church. Wendy and I both received our doctorates at Hansai University by Dr. & Mrs. Cho. Dr. Cho pastors one of the greatest churches in the world and shows us still today that we can change and dreams can come true.

CONTENTS

INTRODUCTION 1

ONE 5
    The Desire for Change

TWO 15
    Are You Conformed or Transformed?

THREE 27
    Your Thinking Determines Your Lifestyle

FOUR..47
    Your Highest Calling Is to Be Like Jesus

FIVE 57
    Capture Every Stubborn Thought

SIX..83
    The Lies We Believe and the Truth that Sets Us Free

SEVEN 99
    Loving Yourself While Pursuing Change

EIGHT 109
    Choices and Emotions

NINE...127
    If You Think You Can—or—If You Think You Can't

TEN 139
    Set Your Mind on Things Above

ELEVEN...153
    You Can Have a Prosperous Soul

TWELVE..183
    Pressing Toward Your Future

THIRTEEN...201
    Detox Your Soul: Bonus Chapter by Caleb Treat

ABOUT THE AUTHORS 227

INTRODUCTION

From Casey

Most of us love a good adventure. Many people dream of being able to travel when they have the time to do so. There is something romantic, exciting, and inspiring about going to places we have not been before. We have travel channels, travel magazines, and travel books; we have travel stores and a whole industry of travel services. Traveling is not always easy or comfortable, but it is one of those things most of us desire to experience. Traveling has a lot to do with imagination, vision, and hope for the good things we will experience on our journey. We make our plans, search the websites featuring our destinations, and dream of what it will be like when we arrive. It's the hope, excitement, and newness that attracts us to traveling. A vision of wonderful places and adventures inspires us to go.

I believe your hope and vision for new things in your life are about to lead you on a unique journey through this book. You and I will go to new places together as we walk through the process of change and renewal. We'll spend a few hours sharing thoughts and feelings and making some changes in our lives. Why are you reading this book? Or any book? Probably, because you believe if you gain a new thought, you can go to new places in your life. If you are thinking and believing better, the things around you will get better. This is the hope that keeps us reading, seeking, and believing for new things in our lives. This hope keeps us on our journey. It is this hope that causes all of us to try to learn and make changes. As we travel together through the next pages, your hope will be rewarded, and new things will start to be birthed in your life.

Is it possible for a person to be raised in unhealthy social and economic conditions but still rise to a better place in life? Can one who has only known divorce and dysfunction in family life build a successful marriage and family that lasts a lifetime? What is the future for one who has been controlled by addictions (food, alcohol, drugs) for years and years? Is there a chance for change in these lives? Or is the future of all people set at birth and we are what we are? Do we have a say in the writing of our story? What if you could change your circumstances and write a new chapter in the story of your life? Would you do it if you could?

I believe you can change. Your story is not yet complete; but if there is a spark of hope and desire in your heart, there are new things ahead for you. I pray that as you read these pages, you will find the thoughts, beliefs, and action steps you will need to experience change in your life. God will give you the grace to change and be renewed in your heart.

I once read an introduction from an author that said, "I apologize for the length of this book. I did not have the time necessary to make it shorter." His point was, it's easier to go on and on talking or writing but never get to the point and say what needs to be said. It takes more discipline and focus to say and do the things that really matter. I hope to be brief, to the point, and say things that can bring change to your life in the next pages.

Wendy has been my girlfriend, best friend, and wife through most of my journey of renewal. We met when I had been saved for just over one year. She will be adding thoughts and truths that will bring renewal to your life. She has a different perspective than I have, and she will help so much in our journey to God's grace that brings change.

From Wendy

At the very beginning of our walk together as Christians, Casey and I were challenged with the amazing revelation of renewing our minds, to think God's thoughts over our negative, defeatist, *you'll never win* beliefs. We immediately told anyone who would listen, starting with our Junior High Youth Group, several small church groups, and then as we began to pastor. Soon after, Casey wrote his first book on renewing the mind.

Now, as we are blessed to go and speak God's Word around the world, we are told testimonies of how that book—and its revelation— changed everything in people's lives. We are excited to bring *Renewing the Mind 2.0*, with our proven life experiences, in a fresh, grace-filled way for today. As you embrace this message, you can have something different in your life. You can walk a new pathway; you can have a better marriage; you can be a better parent; you can be a great friend; you can be a more satisfied, happier person. Years ago we said, "I believe you can," and today we say, "We know you can."

This is not a book about your works. We won't present you with a 21day program and tell you that you will become a *whole new you*. Instead, we will show you how to apply the principles found in God's Word to help you on your pathway to renewal. I pray you capture the underlying spirit of this message—*renewal comes by the grace of God not in our own strength.*

My hope is that you will feel inspired and motivated as you allow the power of God's grace to take you down a new pathway in your life. As you are reading, I would like to encourage you to stop occasionally and say, "Father God, by Your grace, help me to see and do those things that will move me closer to Your will. I can't do it on my own, but with Your help, I can do anything." By holding tightly to the hand of our Almighty God, you will be able to overcome any barriers and walk through any challenges and impossible moments you are facing. None of us can do it alone, but with His grace we can overcome—and have the life we desire.

ONE

The Desire for Change

God gives you the desires of your heart.
—Psalm 37:4

My life for the first twenty years seems to be a dream about someone I knew but can't clearly remember. I can recall how I lived, what I felt, and how I struggled, but it seems like the life of someone else. I felt awkward, uncool, and unable to do the things that would make my life better. I remember despising myself and feeling so bound in my problems that I regularly thought about killing myself. I was trying to medicate my pain with all kinds of drugs and alcohol— legal and illegal. Was that really me or was it someone else? Maybe my life was just a movie I saw or a dream I had, because my life today is so different from my past.

Today I am a husband, father, pastor, and successful person in many ways. Life is fun and full, and at sixty years old my future is bright. I am living the dream in so many ways and still dreaming of great things to come. Sharing how I got from that "other life" to the one I know today is the core message of this book. My prayer is that if you can see and believe the change in my life, you can see and believe it for yourself and your life's circumstances. You are not a victim of some predestined plan to hold you down. You can rise to a new place in life and experience the abundant life God came to give you.

You too can change.

Looking back to my "other life," one event seems to define so much of where I was. It was a typical day in Washington State: gray, cool, and wet. It wasn't a heavy rain, just a steady drizzle that kept everything green and the ground soggy. I had been in Federal

Way, where most of my drug connections lived, and where I typically hung out with friends and medicated my pain. Not much to do and nowhere to go causes people to want another drink or hit or toke—or whatever it takes to forget it all. I could've and should've been excited about my future and had hope, but there was none of that in me; and where there is no vision people perish. Rather than preparing for college and getting excited about a future career, I was trying to avoid the reality of my life. I was spending another afternoon perishing in my lack of vision and my desire to stay numb.

Sometime after dark—time was lost at that point—I decided to head for home. It was a forty-minute drive back to Spanaway, which is located just south of Tacoma, WA. I had about eighteen miles on the freeway and then a few miles on country roads. I'd driven it hundreds of times, but I remember thinking that I really needed to pay attention in order to make it home. I ran my plan through my mind: *Sit up straight, stay under the speed limit of 55, watch my lane, and just get home.* I was doing fine going south on I-5, under the speed limit, staying in the lane, and thinking all was well. Just north of Tacoma, the freeway takes a wide turn from south to southwest and continues on through the city, past the Tacoma Dome. I was being extra cautious as I approached the bend, watching my speed and staying in my lane.

I'm not sure how long it was before I was awakened by lights flashing and a loud voice on a megaphone. I checked my speed, and it was 55. I looked around and could see nothing wrong. Why would I be pulled over? I wasn't speeding. I couldn't be pulled over! I had no license! I had lost it a few accidents, tickets, and DUI's ago. I had drugs in the car and a weapon under the seat. *Oh man, this is bad.* I kept looking around, trying to figure out why the cop was following me. Did he know me? Had he recognized me, or was I just targeted because of past arrests?

Eventually, I realized I was not on the freeway anymore. In fact, I'd been off the road for quite a while. I was stuck in the mud between the north and south lanes on I-5. I was up to the axels in mud, and the rear wheels on the Mustang were just spinning at 55 miles an hour. The speedometer said 55 because the wheels were still turning at that speed, but the car was going nowhere. Mud was spraying up from the rear wheels, and the car was being covered in the wet spray. The extra-wide, Mickey Thompson tires I was so proud of, were throwing water and dirt everywhere.

The cop didn't even want to get close to that mess. He sat in his car and shouted through his megaphone, trying to wake me up. I wasn't totally asleep, but I was not fully conscious either. I was functioning to some degree, but not in touch with reality. When I finally realized what was happening, I turned the car off and got ready for another trip to jail. I knew the routine. I would be handcuffed in the back seat of the cop car, while they searched my car and found drugs, a pistol, and who knows what else. Then off to the Pierce County jail. I was in and out of consciousness through booking, and I woke up the next morning in a cell. How in the world could I let this happen again? I was trying so hard to stay cool and not get in trouble. I really wanted to just get home without another incident.

Looking back now, I wonder how many people are stuck between the lanes of life, spinning their wheels and thinking they are just getting through. Just like me, they are trying not to get in trouble but keep ending up in divorce, bankruptcy, addictions, disease, etc. Maybe this book is the voice shouting from the other car, trying to help them get back on the road, to get beyond medicating the pain and get to the destiny God has for them. Rather than trying to survive and just get through life, we need to make some godly changes.

I remember wanting to change so badly but feeling stuck in negative circumstances and continuing in the same habits again and again. Being angry or discouraged with my situation did not empower me to change. I was still there. So many people don't like where they are but have no power to get themselves to a new place in life.

When I was a teenager, the courts were doing their best to keep me out of prison, but I was not making it easy for them. My probation officer sent me to various counselors and required me to have a job. I guess the thought was to keep me busy, and maybe I would grow up and become responsible. The problem was, at every job and counseling appointment I would meet people just like me. We would end up sharing drugs and medicating the pain of our lives together. Birds of a feather, right?

One job I had was washing dishes at Denny's. They offered me a few more dollars to work the graveyard shift, so I worked from 11 pm to 7 am washing, cleaning, and taking care of the restaurant with a few other employees. I had wrecked a few cars and lost my driver's license, so early one morning as I was walking home, I thought some drugs would make the walk a little better. I took a few things—don't remember what—and set off on my journey of a few miles. As I walked along, I was more loaded than I realized and began to stagger. Probably due to the lack of sleep—graveyard shift is not good for undisciplined people—and also the buildup of drugs in my system, I just staggered beside the road. Eventually, I lost consciousness, stumbled off the shoulder, and fell into a ditch.

Morning traffic was busy, and someone in the "going to work crowd" called the police. They told them they'd seen a teenage boy with long, red hair stumble and fall into a ditch. I'm not sure how long I laid there, because I didn't wake up until I was in jail. The police told me part of the circumstances of how they found me, and my probation officer gave me the rest of the story. Needless to say, no one was happy with me. I lost my job, my parents were at their wits end, and the courts were ready to lock me up for a few years.

How did I get to this place again? It was more than just the drugs. It came from being so unhappy, having no vision and feeling like I had no hope for the future. Millions of people in America and throughout the world struggle with a sense of little or no hope for tomorrow. They see no way out of bad marriages, jobs they don't like, and circumstances where they feel stuck.

Having a happy marriage, fulfilling family, and a successful career seem impossible to people who are like I was. Like me, they're going to work but still struggling with their life. They're walking home every day, but not looking forward to anything. Then they fall in the ditch of negative relationships or personal problems and wake up somewhere they don't want to be. How many wake up in a marriage or a job they do not like, or maybe they become pregnant or addicted, and wonder, *How did I get here, and how do I get out?*

I had no idea that God was hearing the prayers of my little grandma, Roxie, and even in the midst of my pain, He had a plan for my life. If the angels could just keep me alive long enough, there was a bright future for me. The fact is, God has a wonderful plan for every person in this world. We're just trying to find it so we can start living it. His grace is working in us far more than we know.

Many have worked hard all their lives only to find themselves unhappy with their marriage, worried about money, and struggling to find joy in their life. Recently, I worked with several families whose adult children had lost their marriages. Some had lost their children due to depression, addiction, and mental breakdowns. They woke up in the "ditches of life," not knowing where to go. Matthew 15:14 says, "If the blind leads the blind, both will fall into a ditch." I have experienced that truth personally and literally.

One last story will illustrate to you the life I was leading before I found the life God had for me. I don't remember where I'd been that day, but the story was the same as most days. I was high on drugs and drove home to my mother's house in a car I'd borrowed. I parked the car and jumped out, hoping I could get into the house and to my room without my mother noticing anything was wrong. I tried to walk straight and look happy as I went through the door. I said, "Hi, Mom." We exchanged a few words, as usual, and I headed off to my room to hide from the world. I'd made it home safe and sound!

A few minutes later, Mom opened my door, looked in, and asked me what was wrong. Before I could say, "Nothing," or some other fabrication, she said, "Come here." I followed her upstairs to the kitchen window, where she pointed to the car I had driven home. One small problem: It wasn't where I had parked it. It had rolled across the yard and sat idling against the fence. I'm not sure how long it had been there, but it was running through a tank of gas and pushing down the fence in our back yard. Mom said, "What is wrong with you?"

I had no answer for my mom that day. I really didn't know what was wrong with me. Could I not even stop a car, put it in park, and turn the key? Was I so messed up that I could no longer function in the real world? I was embarrassed, depressed, and utterly defeated by my life. Maybe it would be better to die. If there is a God, He would understand, right? Mom called my probation officer, and I knew a new round of trouble was about to begin. Not that it mattered, because my life couldn't get any worse.

Little did I know, that episode was the beginning of my salvation. God had been setting me up all along. Through all the wrong choices I had made, God's grace was working to give me some new opportunities. The probation officer came to my house and told my parents and me that if he told the judge I had violated probation again, the sentence was already set for me to go to prison. The only alternative was to go to a live-in rehab center. Those were my only options: Live-in rehab center for up to a year or prison. It seemed like the worst day of my life but, in fact, it was the first day of my life. Everything was about to change. All the things I thought were impossible for a person like me were about to happen. At my lowest point, I began to look up. Grace will take you from worst to first.

I sat in the entry way of the Washington Drug Rehabilitation Center, waiting to see what would happen to me now. I was scared and nervous but also excited and happy. I knew I could not go on the way I was headed, so maybe now I could make a change. I had no idea how big that change would be. Eventually, I went through a difficult interview, where I cried out for help and had to convince the staff I truly wanted to change. Then I gave up everything I had and committed to following the rules for the next year. By the end of the first day, I wondered if maybe I should have taken the prison option instead! It definitely would have been easier.

Julius Young was the founder and director of the Washington Drug Rehabilitation Center. He was in his late fifties, had grown up on the East Coast, and had spent over twenty-four years in prison.

Having been delivered from heroin addiction and every other evil thing, he had become a Christian and dedicated his life to helping kids like me. In my first group counseling session, Julius said something to me that I hold onto until this day. He said, "Big Red, you can change." Somehow, I believed him. He didn't say, "You better change," or "You have to change." He said, "You CAN change." It was like freedom ringing in my soul. I did not have to be an addict, or scared, or depressed, or suicidal. I could change. And when I changed, every part of my life would change too. Julius became my spiritual father, and for the next few years, he was my mentor and best friend.

I had no idea that five years from that day, I would be married to Wendy and we would be pastors of a church that would become one of the largest in the Pacific Northwest. Now, over forty years later, I'm still growing and renewing. I'm learning how to be a better Christian, husband, father, and grandfather. Julius' words to me, "You can change," are still strengthening my heart and giving hope to my life. I'm not there yet, but I've come a long way, and you can do the same. It's only by God's grace that any of us have a chance to be transformed and experience abundant life—this life that Jesus came to give us. You have the same ability that I have to believe and be transformed by the renewing of your mind.

TWO

Are You Conformed or Transformed?

> Be transformed by the renewing of your mind.
> —Romans 12.2

I find the idea of transformation inspiring. How does a caterpillar become a beautiful butterfly? It's fascinating to watch one of the most dramatic metamorphoses in all of God's creation, a caterpillar—something that crawls along the ground as it is changed into one of the most beautiful of all creatures—one who can fly!

According to *Webster's,* the word *transform* means to "metamorphose, transfigure, convert." These words are defined as meaning: "to change to something different, a major change in form, nature, or function; an abrupt or startling change induced by or as if by magic or supernatural power; a change fitting something for a new or different use."

These words contain powerful meaning for those of us who walk with God. When we understand how transformation works, it is easy to see God's plan. His perfect will is to change us from one form into another; from death to life. God wants to change us from negative to positive; from a depressed person to one filled with joy, from sick to healthy, from financially drained to prosperous. Your transformation begins with the renewing of your mind—exchanging one thought for another. God's grace in our lives empowers us to change and renew.

My transformation began as I was living at the Washington Drug Rehabilitation Center. During my two years there, my life was completely changed. I went from a spaced-out, going-nowhere guy, to Assistant Director of WDRC. I became a Christian. I went to church and prayed the sinner's prayer the first time I attended.

Although I fully embraced my new life, in my heart I didn't really believe I could live that way for the rest of my life. I didn't give myself much hope of life-long change.

As I continued to study the Word of God, I was impressed to read Romans 12:2: "And do not be conformed to this world, but be transformed by the renewing of your mind, that you may prove what is that good and acceptable and perfect will of God." This scripture became the key to my new life in Christ. I saw what God wanted in my life—transformation! That did not mean I had to try to patch up my old life by doing my best; He wanted me to be totally transformed—permanently changed—from who I currently was to the person He—and I—wanted me to be. Grace does not just cover the old—it transforms it!

As I began the process to renew my mind, I first changed one thought, and then another, and another. Time went by and, eventually, I created new beliefs and then a new life. I came to believe that I could live a godly life for more than just one day or one year. I could do this every day for the rest of my life. I knew that I could be transformed!

There are many people who become born again. They come to church, they pray, and then they struggle. It is not as easy as they think it should be. They begin to think, *Well, that didn't work.* They become filled with doubt and frustration. They say to themselves, "I don't get it. I prayed, and I know I'm a Christian. I'm born again, but I'm still the same!" That's when they give up.

A Word from Wendy:
Understanding the Process of Change

If you are having a hard time in the process of renewal, don't immediately think it's because something is wrong. Maybe you are just experiencing a period of growth and the results of making hard choices. When I was first born again, my new pathway wasn't comfortable. I didn't have friends yet, and I was lonely due to my choice to follow Christ. I was in the process of change. I had left my old friends and moved to a new location, starting a new life.

In the midst of your change and renewal, don't get angry or frustrated. Often when you are going through a painful time, you might want to get mad at the people around you. I like to remind myself, *you might not be the only one going through something right now.* It's easy to be upset with others, thinking they did not help you enough. It might be true. I could have pointed a finger and said, "I was a brand-new Christian, and nobody called me. No one invited me to church. Nobody followed up on me. Nobody made sure that I was reading my Bible or learning the principles of God's Word."

It may be true that no one helped me or watched out for me, but God did. God, in His grace, led me to where He wanted me to be. He gave me direction. He became my friend and my comforter. It would be easy to look back at the people who didn't help me and be mad at them, or I can just say, "Thank you, God." I can be grateful for all that He did for me. Even though it was one of hardest times of my life, it was also the best time of my life. Every choice I made to put Him first place in my life brought me strength. Every cry of loneliness brought me closer to Him. Every question I had helped me learn how to get my answers from His Word. His grace was working in me.

When you are going through a change you do not understand, remember, He is right there with you. Spend the time renewing your mind to His Word, and let Him be your strength, your comforter, and your friend.

Have you considered that the dissatisfaction you feel with the negatives in your life just might be God moving you towards something better? Being unhappy or uncomfortable might be the beginning of change for you. When you are done with the old way, you are ready for a new way. Every renewed thought is a step toward the change you and your Father God desire. Many are never told that confessing Jesus as Lord is just the *first step* in living as a Christian. After you're born again, you have to take the next step, which is to be transformed by the renewing of your mind.

God planned for you to live a life that reflects Jesus in your attitude, in your spirit, in your heart, and in your mind. God predestined and established your future to include being like Jesus. We call ourselves Christians because we are to be like Christ. Many times people get frustrated and give up because they don't understand there is a process involved with transformation. They want instant results. The reality is His grace leads us step by step to the new life He has planned for us.

I had to chuckle about the man who told me how he had heard the message on *renewing the mind* and wanted to let me know that it worked! He was renewed! He was amazed at how easy it was! In case you are under the impression that *you have arrived*, I'm quite sure your spouse will help you to understand more clearly how far you are from perfection. Your close friends and family members will be quick to point out that *nobody* has arrived. We are all a work in progress.

As we are on our way to becoming like Jesus, all of our experiences are a part of the molding and shaping of who we are. All of our circumstances—the good ones, the bad ones, the easy ones, and the hard ones—all of our teaching and training adds to who we are becoming. Through it all, remember that God's plan is for you to become like Christ. No matter what you feel, He never leaves you nor forsakes you.

You are not predestined to get rich. You are not predestined to be happy. You are not predestined for a certain position or title, but you are predestined to be like Christ. Obviously, God wants you to prosper, and He wants you to be happy. He wants you to achieve the desires of your heart—that is clearly defined in the Scriptures—but His priority is for you to become like Jesus.

The god of this world is forever fighting for control of your mind. His main arena of attack against you is in your thoughts. We saw it with Adam and Eve, how the devil came to them with just *one thought*.

The repercussions of that one thought are still being felt today.

We see how the devil tried the same tactic with Jesus when he led Him into the wilderness to be tempted (Matthew 4:1-10). Jesus was not exempt from being tempted by the devil, and neither are we. He tried to get to Jesus, and he tries the same tactics with us today. The devil's job is to tempt you by making the things of this world look attractive. He does it by planting a small thought in your mind, just as he did with Adam and Eve. Although Adam and Eve fell for it, Jesus did not. Let's follow His example. He was tempted, but He did not submit to the temptation. He used the Word of God to block every attempt of the devil. When Satan said, "If you are the Son of God," Jesus said, "It is written." He kept His thoughts on God's thoughts.

The problem is that we don't often recognize the tempter when he comes. Our world has become a marketplace of temptation. From the constant television, news, smart phones, Internet, Google, and social media, we are offered temptation on an ongoing basis. The bombardment never ends, and it is well done. There are full-time professionals studying how to get you to buy into their programs, their products, and their way of life.

An advertiser may tell you, "Isn't our product amazing?" But you must believe it, or you won't buy it. If it is found that people are not buying their product, a smart marketer will research how to repackage and re-market that product. After a few magazine ads, TV commercials, and radio ads, that same product will produce entirely different results! What happened? They changed your mind. How did the same product go from unappealing to a *must-have* item? They changed one thought—and it changed what you believed. They flooded your mind with their way of thinking, and suddenly you could not remember why you did not like it in the first place.

This world is under a curse, and those that love the world are buying into the thoughts of the world. You will not be transformed by the renewing of your mind and be able to prove the good, acceptable, and perfect will of God when you conform to the world's way of thinking. How will you get to the perfect will of God? By becoming different, being changed, and being transformed by the renewing of your mind to the Word of God. It's the only way to see real change in your life. You can pray, read, study, build relationships, get a new job, and go to school; but if you are not renewing your mind, you will never move toward God's perfect will for your life.

We see it all the time. You get a new job yet keep the same old problems. You move to a new city and bring the same old problems with you. You get divorced, remarried—and it's the same old problems. It's the same old story because, wherever you go, there you are. You might say, "I'm starting over. I'm getting a new job. I'm going back to school." Okay, but make sure that includes the renewing of your mind, because you are still the same person. If you take your old self, you end up being the same old person with the same old problems. Why? You keep taking that same old attitude and that same old mentality and all those same old beliefs with you. So you're stuck.

Not only are you stuck, but you are becoming conformed, molded, or fashioned to the world. You are moving farther away from God. You don't realize it, but as you become conformed to the world's way of thinking, you are becoming less like Christ. As you are *transformed by the renewing of your mind*, you are moving closer to God. You are moving closer to His good, His acceptable, and His perfect will.

Remember the word *transform* means *to change*, to change from one thing into something different. That's all. It's simple. The movie, *Transformers*, gives a great visual example for us. You have a simple car or truck, and suddenly it begins to change. One moment it is a car and it's just driving along, when all the gears start shifting, and the parts begin moving—and within seconds it has become a huge, fierce, fighting machine. It is no longer a car or truck, but something totally different. It has become something else entirely. That is what God wants to do for you and me. He wants to transform us. His grace is not just covering over our weaknesses or problems—His grace brings real and lasting change.

Do you want to be more like Jesus? I would say most born again Christians have probably desired to be more like Jesus, but it's not a given that they *will* become more like Him. It's a choice. Every time you set your mind on things above, you are moving closer to becoming more like your Lord Jesus.

By the grace of God, you can be conformed to the image of Christ. Let the reality of this sink into your heart. Don't rush past this truth, but think about it for a moment. Your Father God has declared that you will be conformed to the image of Christ. You will be like Christ. It doesn't say that some of us will be conformed to the image of Christ. It doesn't say the really good ones or those who study and pray for an hour each day will be conformed to the image of Christ. It says every one of us, whom He has called His own, will be conformed to His image.

Have you ever heard anyone say that when you become a Christian, God is going to fix everything? I think at one time or another, we have all heard something like that. Sadly, many believe it is true. You thought that when you came to the Lord, gave your life to Christ, and were born again, everything would miraculously change.

Preachers often quote the Bible, where it teaches us, "Therefore, if anyone is in Christ, he is a new creation; old things have passed away; behold, all things have become new." (II Corinthians 5:17). You were told that you would be a brand new person, that the old things would pass away and everything would become new. On a spiritual level, that is absolutely true. When you were born again, you became a new creature in Christ. Yet, here you are—in the same old marriage, same old job, same old finances, same old weight problem, same old attitude problem, same old depression, same old addiction, same old, same old!

What happened? You could be at the beginning of your journey with God or maybe have never heard the message of renewing your mind. Or you may have been deceiving yourself, putting off the inevitable and praying that someday God is going to do it for you. Whatever the case may be, don't fall into the thinking that says, "When you get to heaven, it is all going to be different." God is telling you to get focused. He wants you to get your thoughts right with Him, and as you do, everything else will begin to change in your life.

As you continue to grow and get new God-thoughts, those thoughts will become your new beliefs; and you will begin to believe, *I can be a Christian.* You will embrace the thought: *God is for me.* As you continue to sow God's Word into your heart and mind, you will begin to believe, *God's on my side. God wants me to win. God likes me!*

His grace is always in you, moving you toward His will. When you believe it and embrace it, change happens—renewal happens—and your life gets better. You are not waiting for a miracle or a revival. It won't happen because of a new president or political event. You will see God's abundant life when you embrace His grace and let the renewal process work in your heart and mind.

THREE

Your Thinking Determines Your Lifestyle

As you think in your heart, so you are.

—Proverbs 23:7

Not long ago a close friend of mine told me how he found himself divorced, addicted to drugs, and diagnosed with manic depression. At one time he had been a Christian minister and pastor with a wonderful family. Due to a series of wrong choices, he lost it all. He was depressed, strung out on various drugs, living with someone he didn't really know, and wondering what had happened to his life.

One day, as he was seeking God, he heard this message on renewing the mind. He began to take control of his thoughts and focused his mind on a different way of thinking. Day after day he would deliberately work to set his mind on a new thought. Thoughts like, *I can change*, *I am a successful man*, and *God has a good plan for me*. His soul was being saved. Grace was working in him.

Rather than the self-loathing or destructive and self-pitying thoughts of blaming others, my friend began to see life through a different mindset. Everything in his life did not change overnight, but the change was on. Every time an old thought came into his mind, he replaced it with a new thought. Every new thought was a step towards his new life. It wasn't long before he was back with his wife and children. He returned to ministry, and today you would not know that he was a person who had lost everything, including his mind.

Just as with my friend, your thoughts set the course for your life. Where you set your mind is not only important; it is vital. It is the deciding factor for the kind of life you will live. Adam and Eve learned this truth in the Garden of Eden.

Many theologians believe that Lucifer had full control of Earth at one time (Isaiah 14:12-17). He was the ruler of this world, but God removed him because of the chaos he had created through his rebellion against God—sin was found in him. When the serpent, Lucifer, came into the Garden of Eden, he was looking to find a way back into the world he once controlled. He was scheming to get back his dominion over Earth. Lucifer had been struck down, and someone else had his planet—and his place. Not only that, these humans had something else that the devil did not have; Adam and Eve were made in the likeness and image of God.

God said to Adam in Genesis 1:28, "Be fruitful and multiply; fill the earth and subdue it; have dominion over the fish of the sea, over the birds of the air, and over every living thing that moves on the earth." God gave all authority over Earth to Adam and Eve, and through them, to all of humanity.

At this point, the devil is trying to find a way to gain back what he had lost. He's asking himself, "How do I get access? How do I get control? How do I get back to where I want to be?" His plan is unveiled as he comes to Eve with a thought in Genesis 3:1-5.

"Now the serpent was more cunning than any beast of the field which the Lord God had made. And he said to the woman, 'Has God indeed said, "You shall not eat of every tree of the garden?"'

"And the woman said to the serpent, 'We may eat the fruit of the trees of the garden; but of the fruit of the tree which is in the midst of the garden, God has said, "You shall not eat it, nor shall you touch it, lest you die."'"

"Then the serpent said to the woman, 'You will not surely die. For God knows that in the day you eat of it your eyes will be opened, and you will be like God, knowing good and evil.'"

The serpent did not come to Eve with miracles or grand promises but rather with a subtle thought. He planted one little thought in Eve's mind: *Has God said?* I don't know how long that thought worked in her mind. The Bible doesn't say. Apparently the serpent was very subtle. He brought a little doubt about what God had said. Who knows how long Eve thought about that question, but eventually it led her to the Tree—the Tree of the Knowledge of Good and Evil.

You see, you think it is nothing when the world puts a little thought into your mind. It's no big deal when living together without being married becomes normal. It's no big deal when your sexual identity becomes questioned. It's no big deal when you question or doubt the Bible. It's no problem! It's just a thought.

What did the serpent do? He planted a little thought in Eve's mind. Just a little thought. Then he brought another thought, and another little thought, and Eve started looking at that Tree, and she thought, *You know, maybe God is trying to keep something from us that would make us more like Him.* The Bible says that as Eve looked at the Tree, she saw that it was desirable and would make her wise. As she looked at it, she wondered about all she would gain.

Eve was already made in the likeness and image of God. She already walked with God in the cool of the day. How much wiser can you get? You are hanging out with the Creator of the Universe! But, she had the thought that God was holding back—He was trying to keep something from her. Isn't it interesting that God called it the Tree of the KNOWLEDGE of Good and Evil. God wanted them to understand good and evil, but He didn't want them to gain this knowledge from the world; He wanted them to hear it from Him.

When Adam and Eve ate from the Tree of the Knowledge of Good and Evil, they chose a way of thinking that did not come from God. They rebelled against God. They went their own way and chose their thoughts over the instruction God had given them.

The foundation of all rebellion is choosing to think outside of God's thoughts, which are known in His Word. Lucifer's rebellion caused him to lose his place as ruler of the Earth. Adam and Eve's rebellion caused them to lose their place with God and in His kingdom. Many people today love the Lord, but they choose thoughts that are contrary to God's Word. They prefer a way of thinking that is not scriptural, and it shows up in their life, manifesting in the struggles and problems they experience.

As the story continues, it wasn't long before God was walking through the Garden, as He normally did, and He couldn't find Adam and Eve. He called out to them, "Where are you?"

Adam answered, "I heard Your voice in the garden, and I was afraid because I was naked; and I hid myself" (Genesis 3:10).

God says in Genesis 3:11, "Who told you that you were naked? Have you eaten from the tree of which I commanded you that you should not eat?"

The Lord said to Adam, "Who told you that you were naked?" Remember, God never asks a question because He doesn't know the answer; He asks a question because WE don't know the answer. When God asked Adam where he was, He wanted Adam to look at himself. He wanted Adam to realize, *Yesterday God and Eve and I were chilling in the Garden of Eden. Today, Eve and I are hiding in the bushes.* Now God was asking him, "What happened to you?"

What was God saying to Adam? "Where did you get that thought?" Hiding in the bushes, Adam answered, "Lord, You know we were a little nervous because we realized we were naked, and so we are over here, in the bushes."

God said, "Where did you get that thought? Yesterday you didn't have that thought."

You and I need to know where our thoughts come from. Did you get that thought from the Lord? Did it come from His Word or the world? Some of your thoughts come out of your past failures and fears. Some thoughts come straight from the spirit of this world, from the media and the negative people around us. Some thoughts come out of our flesh, or the old nature.

Isn't it amazing how little children have thoughts and we wonder, *Where did you get that thought?* A small child—maybe two years old, four years old, five years old—and they start lying. The parent asks, "Did you do that?" Their immediate response is no! Where did they get the thought to lie to Mom and Dad? The process we go through today is the same as what Adam and Eve went through in the Garden of Eden. God is saying the same thing to us that He said to Adam: "Where did your thinking come from?"

Where did you get these thoughts: *I'm afraid to share? I'm afraid to commit. I'm afraid to give. I'm afraid to love.* Where did you get those thoughts? You could say: "I got that thought from my dad, who left my mom. I got it from my parents, who went through a disastrous divorce. I got my thinking from watching *Friends* on TV—all ten seasons. I got my thinking from secular school. I got that thought from the newspaper. Where did you get that thought?

If you cannot identify where your thoughts are coming from, you may be living far from the grace of God. When you have no filter in your mind, it will cause you to end up like Adam and Eve, taking your thoughts from the Tree of the Knowledge of Good and Evil. In a sense, you will end up living outside the Garden and losing out on the life God has for you. It's not that God is against you, but when you have chosen to think contrary to His way of thinking, you lose out on His blessing.

There is a wonderful Bible story in II Kings, chapter 5, about a man named Naaman. He was the great commander of the army of the King of Syria. Not only was Naaman a mighty man of valor, but he was also a leper. One day a young Israelite girl was captured and given to Naaman's wife as a servant. This Jewish girl said to her mistress, "If only my master were with the prophet who is in Samaria! For he would heal him of his leprosy." That caused quite the uproar. The King of Syria immediately sent Naaman with a letter to the King of Israel, along with silver, gold, and a few changes of clothing. They wanted the prophet to heal him. That really put the King of Israel on the spot. No pressure, right?

When the prophet Elisha heard about how the King of Israel was reacting, he said, "Please let him come to me, and he shall know that there is a prophet in Israel." This situation was an international incident! It was so talked about and had become such a big deal that Naaman somehow got an idea of exactly how his healing would take place. Unfortunately for him, Elisha had heard something entirely different from God. Instead of making a big production of it, Elisha didn't even personally come out to see Naaman. He sent a servant instead! He had his servant tell Naaman, "Go and dip in the Jordan River seven times." How anti-climactic! Naaman was furious when the prophet did not act according to his thoughts about what would happen. He said, "Indeed, I said to myself, 'He will surely come out to me, and stand and call on the name of the LORD his God, and wave his hand over the place, and heal the leprosy" (II Kings 5:11).

Naaman had a *thought*. He thought God would heal him a certain way, and when that didn't happen, he became angry. He thought the prophet would wave his hand over him and *poof,* the leprosy would be gone. Instead, God asked him to do something that Naaman considered silly: "Go dip in the river seven times." Naaman almost missed his miracle, all because of a thought.

I have spent more time than I want to admit upset with God, because I thought things should happen a certain way, at a certain time. When they didn't happen my way, I was angry and frustrated. I also got discouraged and began to doubt. I had to stop and ask myself, "Where did I get that thought?" It certainly didn't come from the Scripture. It certainly didn't come from the Holy Spirit. I got that thought from my flesh. It came from my own attitude or the world around me. My thinking was keeping me from walking with God in the cool of the day. Do you have a thought that is keeping you from walking with God? Are you hurt or angry, blaming God? Are you discouraged, doubting, or afraid? Negative thoughts often keep us away from the very thing we need—the grace of God.

Have you ever considered the process of how your thoughts become your beliefs? Most of us don't consider the impact of one thought. If we think about it at all, it's easy to pass off as not important. We believe a particular thought doesn't matter; it can't hurt us. We don't see how it will affect our lives. It's just a thought.

You get mad at your wife and think, *She's just hormonal. She doesn't get it and she never will.* Right? Just a small thought. You get frustrated with your husband, and you think, *He's never going to change. I've just got to put up with him because he is my husband.* We don't realize the long-term destruction those little thoughts produce.

One little thought is the beginning of a belief about your husband or wife. You don't see what will happen down the road, but allowing that little thought to take root and grow develops a way of thinking and believing about your spouse. It only takes one little thought to wreak havoc in your relationship and carry you somewhere you never intended to go.

The same applies to your children. You try to raise them by teaching them certain guidelines, which are also *thoughts*. You tell them, "Use your manners. Speak kindly. Look at a person in the eye." You are giving them simple thoughts, which will become the way they believe—and the way they will behave.

Those raised by parents who taught and trained them to have good manners often say, "My mom and dad taught me...." They don't even consciously think about it anymore. It's simply the way they believe and what they do. It has become their lifestyle. Children whose parents never taught them proper manners, a strong work ethic, and respect for themselves and others, often don't know what they are lacking.

Their belief system has nothing godly to help them through life.

The result of not having godly thoughts sown into your life will become a lack of strong beliefs and will eventually affect your lifestyle. Later in life, when you're in your second or third marriage, in the midst of your fourth identity crises, or in the middle of a financial breakdown, you will wonder, *Why is my life so hard?* You don't have the thoughts you need to support the beliefs that will allow you to succeed in life.

When you say to yourself, "This thought doesn't matter," just remember: A thought that you continually process becomes a belief. When you allow yourself to think, *God doesn't heal everybody*, you retain that thought. It becomes a part of your belief system; and when you hear somebody else say it, you instinctively think, *Yes, I believe that too.*

The more you accept a thought as your own, the more it becomes the way you *believe*. Why? You had the thought, you kept it, you endorsed it, you heard others say it, and now it's your way of thinking, your way of believing. Your *thoughts* have now become *beliefs* that are contrary to Scripture. You think you are a believer, living a Christian life, but you have many beliefs that are contrary to the Word of God. Not understanding the conflict, you wonder, *Why isn't God doing more in my life?*

A Word from Wendy: We just don't get sick!

In my younger years, I missed one day of school due to being sick. On that particular day, I came home from school early because my stomach was upset. My mom looked at me and said, "Your brother and your dad are not feeling well either, so why don't you just sit in the front room with them." An hour later I threw up. My mom said, "Okay, so now you're all better."

My mom didn't baby me or tuck me in bed with juice and chicken soup. She didn't pay that much attention to me when I didn't feel well. I know that might offend some, but that was the spirit in which my mom led our household. She believed this: We just don't get sick.

Her belief became my belief.

Casey was raised in a home where sickness was a regular part of life. When we first got married, if he got sick, I would say to him, "Well, honey, we don't get sick." I wasn't very compassionate because I just didn't believe in being sick. Instead of a mindset that accepted sickness as a reason for pampering and medicines, my mom had created a mindset for me and our family: *We don't get sick.*

As Casey and I began learning what the Bible has to say about living in health, we realized there was more to it than how either of us was raised. My mom's, "We don't get sick," and his mom's,

"Here's some medicine," were not the only answers. We knew we had to create a new way of thinking about health based on the Word of God. When we didn't feel well, we began to say what the Bible says. We quoted Isaiah 53:5 (our paraphrase), "By the stripes of Jesus I am healed." We started to renew our minds to the promises for healing found in God's Word.

We all have areas that need renewal, so if you deal with sickness, this is not a judgment. I got strength from my parents about not being sick. Casey and I have lived healthy lives and have taught our children the same concept: *We just don't get sick*. Beyond that, I am talking about the spirit of your mind, about living the way God wants you to live, with a different way of thinking than that of the world. That comes from believing what God's Word has to say about every area of your life and making His Word *what you believe*.

In Philippians 4:8, Paul says, "Whatever things are true, whatever things are noble, whatever things are just, whatever things are pure, whatever things are lovely, whatever things are of good report, if there is any virtue and if there is anything praiseworthy—meditate on these things." The *King James Version* says, "Think on these things." The *Amplified Bible, Classic Edition,* says, "Fix your mind on them."

If you want to have God's thoughts, you must fix your mind on things that are true, noble, just, pure, lovely, of a good report, virtuous. And worthy of praise. Focus on, think on, and meditate on these things. How many of today's television shows line up with this list? How many of the TV shows you watch every day portray qualities that are true, noble, just, pure, lovely, of a good report, virtuous, and praiseworthy? Not very many.

In addition to what we receive from our daily media fix, where else do we get our thinking? When we are depressed or angry; when we get frustrated or full of doubt, where do those thoughts come from? Many times our self-talk is destructive; it is not lined up with pure, true, just, or lovely thoughts. It might be the things others say to us. The words spoken to us by our spouse, children, extended family, friends, or co-workers may not align with God's view of who He has called us to be. Without really *thinking*, we have allowed those words to become a part of who we are.

Much of our thinking is not true, noble, pure, or lovely; and yet, the Bible is clear: We are told to *think on those things.* Why? If you *are* thinking about these things, you are developing beliefs that will move you forward in God's plan for your life. If you *are not* thinking about these things, you are creating a system of thoughts and beliefs that will move you away from God.

Have you ever wondered how a person could serve in a church and attend faithfully for twenty years, then they *suddenly* walk away from the things of God? Thoughts. Their thoughts had been building up. Negative thoughts and thoughts of discontent and frustration were building up, and then one day those thoughts had become their beliefs. BOOM! They just walked away from everything.

When I was young, we always went to one particular gas station because they gave my mom *S & H Green Stamps*. My brother and I would get so excited about a trip to the gas station. As soon as we knew we were going, we would grab the stamp book out of the glove box and start looking. We'd lick the stamps to paste them in the book, and we'd shout, "Four more pages! Three more pages! Only two more pages!" What were we excited about? As soon as we filled the book, we knew we could trade it in for something cool. We were excited about the new toaster or dishes or whatever Mom wanted from the catalog.

Your thoughts are like those *Green Stamps,* and you're filling your book! If your thoughts are negative, you are filling your book and building up towards a heart attack or a relationship break-up. You are *filling the pages* to get your upcoming financial crisis or emotional breakdown—or whatever the result will be from the thought you continually rehearse in your mind. When you look at your life, and *suddenly* there's a crash, a disaster, or a failure, where did it come from? Did it just come up out of the blue? No, you've been collecting stamps for a long time! When your thoughts are good and godly, you are filling your book for good things to come.

Grace is in your life and in your future!

Remember your thoughts become your beliefs, and your beliefs become your lifestyle. You're cashing in sooner or later. How do you keep godly thoughts? Go back to Philippians 4:8, "Whatever things are good, pure, lovely...think on these things." Begin to speak:

•*This is the day the Lord hath made.*
•*Thank you, Father, for a great day.*
•*Jesus, You heal my sickness and cure my disease.*
•*Thank you, Jesus, for loving me.*

There was a popular song back in the early eighties that we sang all the time, and it occasionally goes through my mind today. It goes like this: *"I am healed, and I am whole, from the top of my head to the soles on the tip of my toes. First Peter 2:24 says, I was, and if I was, then I am. I am healed, I am whole, from the top of my head to the soles on the tip of my toes."*

Those are the kinds of thoughts that build beliefs that will keep you alive and healthy as the years go by. In every realm of life, you need to keep godly thoughts in the forefront of your mind. When you think of your spouse, set your mind on thoughts like:

•*Thank You, God, for a wonderful spouse.*
•*Thank You for Your presence in our marriage.*
•*Thank You for keeping my husband/wife strong and healthy.*
•*Thank You for keeping my spouse protected and well.*
•*Thank You for leading him/her at their job today.*

These are the kinds of thoughts that will allow you to hold hands when you're ninety! You will be able to go for a walk around the park and talk about your great-great-grandkids. This way of thinking will give you a life where your family wants to be around you. They will come to visit and want to be part of your life. Do you see the picture I am painting?

How many times has something happened in your life and you thought to yourself, *Yeah, I knew that was going to happen!* Why? You had a thought, and it became the way you believe; then your belief came to pass. You struggle in your marriage and think, *Yeah, I knew it; I told you that husband of mine was a hard head. I told you my wife never got it. I told you!* As much as you may want to deny it, your beliefs created these things in your life.

What if you believe you have a particular DNA or a particular physical make-up, and it's impossible for you to live healthy and fit? You believe it is impossible for you to control your weight because of your DNA. It's your hormones. Your mom told you that you were just like her and her mom. All the women in your family have the same issue. You have accepted the thought—whether it's your family, your heritage, your DNA, or your hormones—and you begin to think it is impossible for you to change that aspect of your life. You just believe it.

Then, because we all look for ways to endorse what we believe, you begin to read up on it. You start your Internet search, you Google it, and go to *WebMD*. You ask friends and family for advice. Everything and everyone has endorsed the theory that you will never be able to be healthy and fit. You know Google can't be wrong! They have confirmed what you already knew! It has become fact in your mind, and you believe it.

For the next twenty years, you continue believing you can't be healthy. Due to the hormone problem, you've got the extra weight to deal with, and that takes your blood pressure off the charts. What do you suppose is going to happen when you're sixty? What do you suppose is going to happen when you're eighty? You probably won't make it to sixty-five! Why? You believe you can't be healthy!

Over and over Jesus said to the disciples, "What you believe will come to pass." Isn't that right? In Matthew 9:22 He said, "Your faith has made you well." That is what we all want to have in our lives. We want our faith to make us whole. The same principle can also bring those things we don't want into our lives. This principle is true for both the negative and the positive. When we allow negative thoughts and beliefs into our hearts and minds, we get that negative thing. We have *faith* in it. We *believe* for it. When we believe for the positive thing, that is what we have as well.

For over forty years I've been saying this:

If you renew your mind, you can renew your life!

If you can change a thought, you can change your life!

I mean *any* part of your life. You can change your health. You can change your finances. You can change your relationships. You can change how you look; how you feel, how you get up in the morning, and how you face every challenge you encounter. You *can* change!

FOUR

Your Highest Calling Is to Be Like Jesus

You are predestined to be like Him.

—Romans 8:29

Everything within me says, "I can change, I can be better, I can overcome these negatives in my life," but then I struggle to make it happen. Is there really a way to change and see improvement in our lives? I believe there is. Years ago I started on a journey to radically change my life. Although I felt the frustration of being unhappy with myself, I learned that frustration would not bring change. I've been there. You've been there. We have all felt stuck, not liking what we do but doing the same thing over and over again. Like a hamster on a wheel or being caught in a maze, we struggle to break free, yet never quite reach our goal.

How often have you heard yourself or someone you know use the phrase, "I was born this way?" Maybe you've heard yourself say, "This is just the way I am." Although this is the easy answer to those things you don't know how to deal with, is it the truth? Were you destined to struggle, never to rise above your current level of life? Are you permanently stuck in the life you have now?

You and I share a common desire. We want change in our lives. I think that is true for most people. No matter what class, status, or place you are in your life, there is something you want to change or make better. There are thoughts, emotions, and behaviors that you are not happy with. You want them to go away or change, but as we all do, you struggle with how to make that happen. Even though you tell yourself, "I can change," years go by as you continue in the same old rut. The American dream says, "You can rise to success in life," but so many never do. Even the Bible says that *you can put on a new man* (Ephesians 4:24).

With a dream of something more, many hope an outside force like the government, a union, or their company will make their lives better and bring change to their circumstances. Some try to find their change in a pill, an exercise program, or a new diet plan. The promises of programs, infomercials, or politicians bring hope for a moment but often fall flat in the end. For those who trust in God, there is another answer.

The change you long for happens as your mind is renewed to the Word of God and the thoughts of God. Did you know that as a born again Christian, you are predestined to be like Jesus? The Bible says in Romans 8:29, "For whom He foreknew, He also predestined to be conformed to the image of His Son, that He might be the firstborn among many brethren." It is God's plan for you to become like Jesus. If you are like Jesus, it follows that you can have a new way of thinking and a new way of living—*you can change*.

When you accepted Jesus as your Lord and Savior, your spirit was completely made new. However, your *soul* (mind, emotions, and will) and your *body* were not. Those areas of your life are in the life-long process of renewal. Your soul is saved as you renew your mind to the Word of God. Your body will be saved when the Lord returns, and in the twinkling of an eye, you shall be changed. Your mortal body will put on immortality, your corruptible flesh will put on incorruption, and you will rise to meet Him in the air (I Corinthians 15:52-54).

The "saving of your soul" is also called the renewing of your mind. When you make Jesus your Lord, the Bible says you are saved; you are born of God and on your way to Heaven. This birth takes place in your spirit and is eternal. Unlike your spiritual rebirth, the saving of your soul takes place in the realm of the mind. It happens as you exchange your worldly thinking for the thoughts of God, and changing your thinking will literally change the way you live. James says that the Word of God we receive is able to save our soul (James 1:21).

We all have things in our lives that we know should change: things we should stop doing, things we should start doing, things we should do better or do more of—every one of us. We may think that we can't overcome our problems because we are just not right with God. We keep trying to get better by getting saved again and again. In some churches, you can get born again every Sunday. In fact, the pastor encourages it. Rather than getting born again...again or rededicated on a weekly basis, you need to believe that your relationship with God is eternally secure.

Salvation is a gift. We cannot earn our salvation from God, but He does tell us we need to *work it out*. Paul said to the church at Philippi, "Work out your own salvation with fear and trembling" (Philippians 2:12). I like how the *Amplified Bible, Classic Edition*, says it: "Work out (cultivate, carry out to the goal, and fully complete) your own salvation." We are to *cultivate, meet the goal*, and *bring to completion our salvation*. He is saying, "You are a Christian—now live your Christian life." What does it mean to fully live this Christian life? I believe Paul was telling us, "Don't just get saved and then wait until you get to Heaven to experience God's blessings. Work out your salvation now, while you are living on Earth. Your spirit is saved—born of God—now let your soul be saved."

I'm sure you have had someone tell you they are a Christian, and you said to yourself, "No way!" Right? They didn't talk like a Christian. They didn't act like a Christian. They seemed to always be the one who ended up in every disaster in the world. They lived just like the world, and even though they said they were a Christian, you couldn't tell them apart from non-Christians. Why is that? Because they haven't worked out their salvation. Just by looking at them and watching how they talk and how they act, there is no way to tell they are a Christian.

Why don't more Christians have the abundant life they dream of? Why are they not *working out* their own salvation? That's a great question, and the answer will bring you to the brink of discovering a whole new way of life. It's the key to the message of this book.

The key component of working out your salvation is the *renewing of your mind*. If you can renew your mind, you will be able to walk in God's abundant life. As you renew your mind to God's Word, you will learn how to live a *saved* life, an abundant life. The saving of your soul will make a great difference in your everyday life.

Many people believe in Jesus, but they never really change the way they think. Have your thoughts about your marriage, finances, family, and career changed since you were saved, or are they still the same? Do you watch a family member go through an ugly divorce and think, *That's just the way life is*? Do you live a *barely-get-by* life and feel satisfied making the minimum payment on your five credit cards? And do you feel pretty good as long as your kids aren't as bad as the other kids? Those thoughts do not line up with God's Word.

It is possible to love the Lord but still think like the world. Your unrenewed way of thinking accepts as *normal* many things that are *not normal* for a born-again believer. When your mind is unrenewed, you do not see that there is something more for you, so you are willing to accept less than what God has for you. So many haven't realized that the promises found in God's Word offer a higher way of living for every believer.

The answer to your ongoing struggle to change your life is simple: The grace of God will help you to renew your mind. You won't be able to do it on your own—and He cannot do it for you—but He wants you to succeed and become the person He created you to be. With His help, you *can* do it. By grace you are saved—spirit and soul—in every part of your life!

How many have resisted becoming a Christian because they felt they would lose more than they would gain? Funny how that one thought will keep people from God's greatest gift. I thought for so long that if I committed myself to Him, I would miss out on so much fun in life. That is the lie the devil uses to keep so many from the kingdom of God. It's common to hear people say, *"As soon as I am done sowing my wild oats I will commit to being a Christian."* They say to themselves, "If I get saved, all the fun is over. I need to do all the fun things I can first, and then I will get saved." What they don't realize is God will never take something good from them or keep them from a better life. Instead, He wants to give them abundance, success, and the highest kind of life.

You may be one of those who believe God's ways are irrelevant to your life today. The world is full of those who believe the Bible is archaic. They think church is a mausoleum filled with cranky people who have nothing better to do than believe in myths. The truth remains: God has a much higher way of living, and it is available to every person. He has more for us than most of us ever experience. Just as Adam and Eve lost the freedom and privileges available in the Garden of Eden through rejecting God's thoughts, you and I miss out on His higher life in the same way.

How can you experience life in a way that is so much better than that which you now know? It will only happen when you accept God's thoughts as true. When you receive what the Bible teaches, you are choosing the thoughts of God. Believe His thoughts. As you apply them, you will begin your journey to a higher level of living. Every area of your life will be changed. You will increase and succeed in your relationships, in your family life, in your business or career, and even in your health. The life God offers is higher in every way. It is the highest way of living.

A Word from Wendy: Your New Life

It's a unique pathway as you learn to walk with Christ and begin to renew your mind. As with any new path, it seems unfamiliar and lonely at first. God may ask you to leave behind familiar activities and relationships. That might be easy for you, or you may struggle, not wanting to walk away from what you have always done or the people you have been with. There could be a part of you that thinks, *Wait—all my friends are going to be there. I can be comfortable there*. But, you're not. The Spirit of God is speaking to your heart. He is leading you, teaching you, and training you in His new path for your life. Often your new path will lead you away from the old ways of your past. As you keep your spirit open to hearing His voice, you won't be comfortable in the same places and situations as you were in the past.

You can ignore God's leading in your life. It's your choice. If you choose to ignore His thoughts, recognize that you may lose that moment of grace in your life. When God gently comes to you and says, "Don't act like this; don't talk like that; don't go into this environment or be involved with this action;" be quick to listen and obey. He speaks in a still, small voice when bringing His freedom into our lives. Stay open to listening when He speaks and be ready to obey His leading.

How many have come to the Lord and said, "I believe in Jesus," and that is the last thought about God they ever have. They don't seek to find out if there is more to this Christian life. They don't realize that to walk with God doesn't take just one new thought but rather *a whole new way of thinking.* You say you want change in your life, but how will change actually happen? Change comes from new thoughts, a new way of thinking, a new perspective on life. You need God's way of thinking, His perspective, because His ways are higher than your ways, and His thoughts are higher than your thoughts (Isaiah 55:9).

One day as I was praying, I said, "God, how can I ever live in Your ways? How am I ever going to get my life in line with what your Word says I can have?" I felt God said, "Just start with My thoughts, and My ways will come automatically." You say you want the ways of God to have preeminence in your life. You want God's way in your marriage, in raising your children, in your company, business, and finances. What are you willing to do to get the thoughts of God? Are you prepared to study the Word of God and renew your mind? Will you submit your thoughts to His higher thoughts?

How are you going to increase your finances? I promise you it is not going to be through a government loan program or your credit card. You are not going to borrow your way into prosperity. It is not going to happen in this natural world. However, if you can get a higher thought, you can get to a higher place financially. Your financial freedom starts with your new way of thinking. Your new way of thinking will bring you into the higher way of life, which God has ordained for you.

Why do so many marriages fail? One or both of the partners will get stuck on a thought about the person or the situation, and they will think, *I'm not going to change my mind.* If one or both in the marriage won't go for a higher thought, then you can't have a stronger relationship. If you are not willing to change your thinking, your relationship is doomed to fail. On the other hand, a different thought about your spouse and your marriage will cause you to have a different marriage relationship.

If you can get God's higher thought's, you will have a higher life. If you get a higher way of thinking, you will have a higher way of living.

It all starts with a thought. One thought can change everything.

FIVE

Capture Every Stubborn Thought

> Bring every thought into captivity to the obedience of Christ.
> —II Corinthians 10:5

Do you remember Dr. Dobson's book, *The Strong-Willed Child*? Have you seen or maybe even raised a stubborn child? At times, it seems like every child is strong-willed! They get something in their minds, and they just do not want to obey. It's a struggle, but as a parent what do you do? You teach and train them how to think right and how to behave right. A good parent helps their child learn *how to think*. The Bible teaches us in Proverbs 22:15, "Foolishness is bound up in the heart of a child; The rod of correction will drive it far from him."

What happens when a child does not have anyone to help them overcome their foolish ways? That child becomes a foolish adult. Isn't that true? How many of us have seen the result of foolish thinking manifested in someone's life? Our juvenile detention centers and prisons are full of those who did not have anyone willing or able to help those individuals deal with their wrong thinking.

Children who hang on to foolish ways of thinking become adults with problems. They can't keep a job; they can't maintain good relationships; they don't know how to live in a manner that is satisfying and healthy. Their soul is not prosperous, so they can't prosper. As hard as they may try, those foolish, stubborn thoughts are the strongholds that weigh them down. Those thoughts must be broken if they want to live the life God has for them.

Second Corinthians 10:3 tells us, "For though we walk in the flesh, we do not war according to the flesh." Although we live in the natural world, many of our problems are not natural or physical. Many times we want to fight whatever natural situation that tries to overwhelm us. We charge ahead, thinking we can win the battle alone or with a few of our friends and family—in the natural. Most people never overcome the problems they face because they don't know: *The problem you are dealing with does not come from what is happening around you in the natural realm; it comes from the spiritual and mental realm.* It's not in the natural or physical realm but in the mental and spiritual realm that the real battle is won.

Verse 4 says, "For the weapons of our warfare are not carnal but mighty in God for pulling down strongholds." I believe this passage of Scripture holds one of the most important keys to the renewing of our minds. God is telling us our weapons are not natural weapons. They are not the things we can do on our own. He's telling us, "This battle you are in isn't a natural fight. It's not a fight you can win with your flesh."

The weapons of your warfare are not carnal—they are not of the flesh. They are not physical weapons, but they are mighty in God for pulling down strongholds. The weapons of your warfare have been handcrafted by Him. These weapons are spiritual, and they come from the Spirit of God. They are inside you, and they are perfect for pulling down strongholds—the *strongholds* in your mind.

Verse 5 continues by telling us, "Casting down arguments and every high thing that exalts itself against the knowledge of God, bringing every thought into captivity to the obedience of Christ." The *strongholds* Paul is writing about here are arguments—the *King James Version* calls them, *imaginations*—knowledge that is contrary to or against the Word of God. This is the true battle we are fighting against—thoughts that *are not* from Christ. The fight we are to engage in is about pulling down arguments, knowledge, and thoughts that are not obedient to Christ—thoughts planted in our minds that disagree with the Word of God.

Paul is writing to impress upon us a crucial truth: *The strongholds you allow in your mind will decide your destiny. If you win the battle for your mind, you can have God's will; but if you lose this fight, you will lose much of what God has for you in life.*

In defining what a stronghold is, I'm going to use the words—*stubborn thoughts*. Think about the time you had a thought that you knew wasn't right. *You* didn't even like it. You didn't want to think that way, but it seemed so hard to stop. That's a stronghold. It's that thought that has a strong hold on your mind, and you just can't seem to shake it.

Strongholds are those arguments—those thoughts—that need to be brought into *obedience* to Christ. These are the thoughts that must be captured. *Every* one of them. Even those stubborn thoughts that just will not go away. Have you ever had one of those thoughts? You know you shouldn't think that way, but it's stubborn, and it just hangs on. You got angry about something, and you thought to yourself, *Just let it go. Leave it alone. It's not worth being mad about*. But within a few minutes, you were thinking about it again. You know you should move on and forget about it, but it just keeps coming back. You keep thinking about it and, as you do, you get more and more upset. Then you start telling other people about it, and you say things that you know you shouldn't be saying. You end up saying to yourself, "Why did I do that?" It's a stronghold. It's a stubborn thought that won't let go.

What you need to do is pull that stronghold down. I know, it is easier to say it than it is to do it, but be encouraged; Paul is telling us, "You can do it!" Winning this battle is possible. If you face the situation God's way, He will empower you and help you to win this battle. You will win! You will be able to capture every thought, bring it into obedience to Christ, and go on with what God has for you.

We have all heard of people who have gotten stuck on certain thoughts, and the toll it takes in their lives. How many stories have we heard about a married man or woman who finds their old girlfriend or boyfriend on social media, only to begin an adulterous relationship? How in the world does that happen? Strongholds. A thought. One thought gets in your mind. It begins by remembering when you were seventeen, and you still looked good. You were the football hero, and in those days you could still see your shoes when you looked down. Your life was so awesome, and you were in love! The more you think about how great those days were, the more you just know you have to call Sally. You just want to see what she's doing. That thought is the beginning of a stronghold, and it will alter the course of your life if you let it.

Maybe for you, it's depression. Your thoughts become focused on a failure in your life. Other things have gone wrong in the past, and you can move on; but then, there's that *one thing*. You can't forget how you dropped out of school, left your spouse and went through a divorce, had an abortion, and quit a certain job. Now you look back and think, *Why did I do that? What was I thinking?*

That one thought starts to become a weight, a stronghold in your mind. Depression becomes associated with that thought. You may think, *It's over. It's done. I'm going to move on. God forgave me.* You know it's time to move forward, but the next day the same thought is back. Maybe it's a place you visit that reminds you or it's a song you hear, and the thought is right there. It keeps coming back, and it just won't leave. It's one *stubborn thought* that keeps pulling you down.

Some have a stronghold in the area of addiction. In their mind they think, *if I just use that drug, I'll feel better. If I just have a little drink, it will take the edge off and make me feel better.* Your thought that the addiction makes you "better" starts controlling you. Your thinking starts weighing on you—it just won't leave you—and you try to convince yourself, *That's not true. I don't believe it will make me feel better. I know what's going to happen. I've been there before, and I don't want to go there anymore.* But, unless you get real with yourself, that stubborn thought will continue to control your life.

Maybe your thought is, *It doesn't matter anymore. It doesn't matter what I do; I'm not going to get a raise. It doesn't matter if I work hard; I'm not ever going to get a promotion. Doesn't matter if I come to work early and stay late. No one notices. It just doesn't matter.* In your marriage you may think, *It doesn't matter if I tell my spouse they are the best, because they just give me the same old, uh huh. It just doesn't matter.* As soon as that thought takes root, it becomes a stronghold in your mind, and then it starts running your life. It becomes your *go-to* response every time you face that situation.

Paul said in II Corinthians 10:4, "The weapons of our warfare are not carnal but mighty in God for pulling down strongholds." At the end of the day, this is the warfare that matters. It's not about political parties. America isn't going to fail because of politics. Beliefs and controversies over domestic issues are not the problem.

Immigration, health care, and foreign policy are real issues, but they are not what will bring us down. Our issues are not the things politicians use to try to get attention. As a people, we will fail because of our thoughts. Our biggest problem is what we think and believe, because "as he thinks in his heart, so is he" (Proverbs 23:7). When strongholds take over your life, you do things you never thought you would do. Addictions, marriage failures, financial crises, even racial prejudices come from strongholds in our minds.

Let me ask you a question: Have you ever found yourself in a situation where you have said or done things that you never thought you would say or do? Have you said things to your spouse you never thought you would say? You know what I'm talking about. You find yourself in a situation you don't want to be in. You default to bad behavior, depression, or some other negative choice. Then, when things go wrong, you end up thinking, *How did that happen?*

It starts with a negative thought that becomes a stronghold. You messed around with a thought, and you let that idea stay in your mind. When that thought takes hold and starts running your life, you're headed for a crisis. I don't mean you'll lose your salvation. You're still a Christian, but in order to be transformed by the renewing of your mind, you must win this battle! You must defeat the stronghold. One thought can make the difference in your life. One thought.

The strongholds in your mind will bring you to the brink of things you never thought would happen in your life. You have the ability to fight against them, to rise above them and win the battle. The good news is, you are not alone in the battle. Every battle needs a plan in order to succeed, and our strategy is found in the Word of God.

Powerful Steps to Pulling Down the Strongholds in Your Life:

Step #1: Awareness

In the midst of doing something that doesn't help you, stop and ask yourself, "Why am I doing this?" Most of us never stop to figure out why we do the things we do and why we don't do the things that would make life better.

Second Corinthians 10:5 tells us that we are to *bring every thought into captivity.* You start to capture every thought by becoming aware of what you're thinking. To win the battle and pull down the strongholds, you need to grab ahold of every thought. Capture means: to get control of, gain control by force, take prisoner.

Do you know what is really going on in your head? Most of us would say, "Of course!" I would have to challenge you to take a closer look. Become aware of what you're thinking. If you are daydreaming about old love affairs, it's not healthy for your current marriage. If you spend the day dreaming about your next vacation while you're at work, it's not going to help you get that next promotion. If you come home and watch three hours of television every night, it's not going to add any energy or vitality to your goals.

How many times has someone asked, "What are you thinking about?" The standard answer is...*nothing!* For some, that is the absolute truth. They have no idea where their thoughts are going. But, if you want to change your life, you need to become aware. Ask yourself, "What am I thinking about right now? Where is my mind going? What are my thoughts?" The Bible says in Proverbs 23:7 that *as a man thinks, so is he; or, as a woman thinks, so is she*.

I know we use "Nothing!" as our easy answer when asked what we are thinking about, but I hope you don't believe that it's true. You are always thinking about *something*, right? For instance, you are sitting in church on a Sunday morning, it's 12:40 pm, and the preacher is preaching. You're thinking, *I shouldn't think about lunch. I'm not going to think about hamburgers today. I'm definitely not going to have a cheeseburger with bacon. Nope, not going to think about that. I'm not having the extra cheese with an extra patty. Not going to think about that. I will not have fries with my burger! I probably won't have a chocolate milkshake—not going to do it.* Then you start wondering if you left the stove on after you made your eggs, all while saying, "Amen, Pastor!" It is all going on in your head while the preacher is preaching. You are always thinking about something.

What about the day you thought, *Maybe I should fast today*? You ended up eating three times what you usually eat! Why? Because the minute you think, *Don't think about eating,* it is all you can think about. You just can't get it out of your mind. You try to focus on something else. You tell yourself to *think about something else. Focus on thoughts of God,* but you end up eating the food because you can't get it out of your head.

Do you think more about your problems or your promises?

You're always thinking about your money, your marriage, your kids, and your job. Are you thinking about those things in a positive or a negative way? Are you aware of how much more you think about your problems than you think about the promises of God? Problems or promises? If we could weigh the balance of your thoughts, which ones would tip the scale?

Step #2: Focus

Focus your mind on the thoughts of God. When I say, *renew your mind*, I'm not talking about positive thinking. There are many *positive thinking* gurus in the world. In spite of all their positive thinking, when their lives are in crisis, they still have the same troubles everyone else has. Renewing your mind isn't about just being a happier, nicer person; it is about thinking the thoughts of God— being a godly person.

Isaiah 55:9 tells us that God's thoughts are higher than our thoughts and God's ways are higher than our ways. Focus on *His higher thoughts* if you want *His higher ways*. Focus on His *better thoughts* if you want a *better life*. Focus on His *richer thoughts* if you want a *richer existence*.

Why do you go to church every week? I hope you come to learn the Bible. As a pastor, I don't read newspapers or magazines to my congregation. There's no power in newspapers or magazines. I don't read nice poetry. There's no power in nice poetry. I read and teach the Scriptures. Why? The Word of God is alive and powerful (Hebrews 4:12). There is substance—life-giving power—in the Word of God. Positive thinking is mankind's attempt at using the principles of God to overcome their problems. Only the Word of God contains the power to change your life. Thinking and living God's thoughts is much more than just positive thinking.

One way I have learned to focus my thoughts is to have a *go-to thought* prepared for every circumstance. Then I am ready for whatever comes my way. What are a few *go-to thought's* for situation's that may occur in your life? Let's imagine that your boss comes to you tomorrow and says, "I'm sorry, we have to let you go. We're downsizing the company, and we aren't able to keep you on the payroll. I am giving you your two-week notice." What is your *first* thought? If you focus on the thoughts of God and you know His promise in Philippians 4:19, then you will say, "My God shall supply all my need according to His riches in glory by Christ Jesus."

You don't start crying or worrying. You don't get drunk at lunchtime while trying to figure out how to tell your spouse. You have a *go-to thought* that takes you to a higher level. If you are conformed to the world, you might get mad or depressed. If you are transformed by the renewing of your mind, you move closer to God's perfect will. You think to yourself, *I believe I am going to make more money in my next job.* You can be thankful that you are moving toward your destiny. You can say, "Thank you for being a part of my life," and mean it, because you have a higher way of living. You have a *go-to thought*, a way of thinking that moves you forward when faced with a challenge.

What about when you get the call from your doctor, who says, "Your blood test appears to have elevated protein levels. We're concerned about it, and we need to do more testing to make sure you don't have cancer." What's your *go-to thought*? Do you call everybody you know and say, I've got cancer! "I've got six months to live!; I knew it was going to happen to me!" Is that your *first* thought? Or you could say, "Thank you, doctor. I appreciate your input. You know I'm a Christian right? Well, I believe Jesus bore my sickness and carried my disease. I just want you to know I'm not worried because I believe that by the stripes of Jesus I was healed."

A Word from Wendy: My Phone-Call-Moment

We all have challenging situations that come into our lives. Although we may not know when and how those challenges will arrive, we *can* know that we're prepared for them. I call it a *phone-call-moment*. I received a *phone-call-moment* the day my doctor called to say, "You have cancer." It was an ordinary Tuesday afternoon, and I had just gotten home from work when the phone rang. The furthest thing from my mind was getting that phone call. As soon as the doctor said those three words, the fight was on. I could have panicked, but I immediately knew I had to make myself focus on the Word of God that was planted in my heart and mind.

We will all experience a *phone-call-moment* at some point in our lives. That moment of distress when the old pathway of doubt and fear wants to rise up and take over. Instead of letting fear-filled thoughts race across your mind—you can have another way of thinking, one that says, "I'm not going down that pathway of fear. I'm going to trust in You, God." You may not fully understand it—you might even be a little bit afraid—but you put your trust in Him.

When I got the call, I had to sit very quietly for a few moments, and then I said, "God, I need help right now. Father God, I believe I will live a long, prosperous life." I had to command myself to think the thoughts of God, because my mind instantly wanted to go down a very dark pathway. I had lost my mom to cancer. It was a very slow, painful process, and I witnessed firsthand the devastating effects of cancer in her body. When I heard the word *cancer*, my mind went straight to that horrible moment from my past. Also, I had gone through eleven long months of Casey's chemotherapy treatment for Hepatitis C. I saw the results of chemotherapy on his body. Immediately my mind was racing down those pathways, and I wanted to be afraid.

As I focused my thoughts and quieted my heart and mind, I asked God to help me be strong. I asked Him to help me fight this battle based on the decision I had already made—to submit my life to His ways. I reminded Him—and myself—*I am a woman who will live a long, prosperous life*. I did not allow fear to dominate me. I refused to go down the pathway of seeing my mom in her last moments of life. I would not focus on remembering how Casey looked as he lost a lot of his hair and got so thin. Do not focus on the sad parts of your history or let fear overwhelm you, instead, let your heart be filled with His grace and ability—with the strength of His Word.

Don't think I am saying that negative emotions will not try to overwhelm your senses. They will. While you are declaring your trust in God's promises, you will probably experience fear and doubt. Every negative thing you have experienced or heard relating to your situation will begin to go through your mind. Your emotions will want to take control. God is not afraid of your emotions, neither is He offended or worried when you talk to Him from an emotional, vulnerable position. He created you to have emotions. Just don't let your emotions control your situation.

When Casey came home that day, he looked at me and knew something was wrong. My husband adores me, so of course, his first thought was, *No, not my wife; not my best friend.* The people who love you will also have to fight thoughts of fear and doubt. I'm so grateful Casey stood strong beside me as we prayed, worshiped, and thanked God that His promises were working in my body.

Today I am healthy, restored, and my body is 100 percent cancer-free. Was it easy? No. But it was possible. My healing didn't come from a memorized list of scriptures or knowing a whole book of the Bible but from a core belief of who God is and what He has done for me. Your strength, healing, provision, and all you need will come as you focus on His promises and trust in the God of love, grace, and kindness.

When you can't focus your thoughts on the promises of God, all you have left are the thoughts which are conformed to the world. Your emotions—how you feel about the situation—can rise and fall. We all have emotions that try to take over, but if you can focus your thoughts on how God has already fought the battle for you, you have already won.

What do you do when your child's school calls and says, "Johnny has been in an accident"? Do you start crying? Do you immediately let fear take over and begin to think the worst? Or do you say, "I have prayed for that child from the moment he was conceived, and I know his steps are ordered of the Lord. I know my child will be fine."

These things are not easy, but what's the alternative? Do you really want to depend on the thoughts of the world to see you through? What is the result of thinking like the world? Worldly thinking brings depression, anxiety, addiction, sickness, and all the problems we see people go through every day. How can we, as Christians, be different? We will only be different from the world if we think differently. We will only have something different if we can capture every thought and bring it into the obedience of Christ.

Step #3: Practice

To have something new in your life, you have to practice it until it becomes a part of you. Your new way of thinking will not feel right at first; in fact, it will feel extremely uncomfortable. And here's the problem: We don't like things that are uncomfortable. New shoes are uncomfortable. A new chair is uncomfortable. A new job is uncomfortable.

You attend a new church, and it's uncomfortable. People will ask you, "How did you like the church service?" You can't explain it, but you think, *Something wasn't right.* They had an uplifting time of praise and worship, powerful prayer, and the teaching was practical, but you weren't comfortable. Why? It's new. After attending for a while, you begin to see a few familiar faces, you find your favorite seat, learn the words to the songs—and it starts to become comfortable. Now it feels good. Did they change anything? No. What changed? You changed.

Your wife moves the furniture all around, and you say, "Wait, I can't see the TV. There's a glare on the TV screen. That is not going to work!" Is it really a problem? No, it's just that now it is different. It's uncomfortable. For some reason, we like to avoid being uncomfortable at all costs. That's one of the biggest problems with renewal. We avoid the new thought because the new thought makes us feel *uncomfortable.*

Did you know that people who have been poor and suddenly make more money than they've ever made before will lose it quickly? The guy who was barely making it wins the lottery! He's an instant multi-millionaire. What does he do? He does something to get rid of it as soon as possible! He has an inner drive to get back to what's comfortable. He is more comfortable being poor. Why? That's what he's used to. As a poor man, he can complain about how hard life is. He can blame rich people. He can talk about what he would do if only he had the money. As soon as he got more money than he ever had had, he unconsciously thought, *This is so uncomfortable!*

I should get rid of this!

Did you know that some people actually like being sick? You like being sick more than you like being healthy because you have something to talk about when you are sick. You tell your friends, "You know what the doctor gave me yesterday? Let me tell you about my latest prescription. I had this new pain, and you'll never guess what Google said about it!" You can't wait to tell everyone about your new pain because it gives you something to talk about. It is your *go-to* conversation, and it's comfortable.

A stronghold is not only a stubborn thought; it is a comfortable thought. Many times the things you are most comfortable with are the hardest things to get rid of. Maybe you have an old robe and your spouse has been trying to get rid of it for years. You say, "No, you can't get rid of it! It's my favorite!" It's ugly, it's worn out, it's looking bad, but you are comfortable wearing it. You need to hang onto it just one more year—and then another and another.

It's those old slippers. The dog doesn't even want to sniff those things! They're so comfortable you can't let them go. It's your favorite old chair. It's so comfy. You don't want to look underneath and see what's in that chair, but it's your chair. It's just so comfortable. It's hard to let go of that which makes you comfortable. Sometimes, especially as you get older—and I'll let you define what older is—it becomes harder to move on. You don't want to let go. It's hard to change because you are comfortable where you are.

A Word from Wendy: You've Got Holes in Your Slippers

Like a comfortable pair of old slippers, we often don't realize areas we need to renew until those areas slap us in the face. You don't notice that those slippers are full of holes! You put your foot up—and boom!—everyone else sees the holes.

One evening when Casey and I were still dating, we were at a party with many of our friends. I was having a great time, laughing and talking, when someone said something about Casey. I responded with a sarcastic comment. That was my standard response. When somebody else made another comment, I again said something sarcastic about Casey.

During the drive to my home, Casey pulled the car over and said, "Can I ask you a question?" I was all jovial and happy from being at the party and had no idea there was anything wrong. He asked, "Why did you say that about me?" I didn't have a clue what he was talking about. Again he said, "Why did you say those words about me?"

I responded, "What words?"

He said, "Well, you said..." and he repeated my comments. What I had said was a sarcastic, mean-spirited comment about him.

I looked at him and said, "I did what?" I honestly did not know what he was talking about.

Casey said, "I don't want that type of communication to be a part of our conversation. I don't want us to talk like that to each other."

I said, "I didn't even realize what I was doing." I had something right in front of me to renew my mind about and didn't even know it. Like those old slippers with holes in them, I had become so comfortable in the negative way of communication I had been raised with, that I didn't see it. It was just the way we talked in my home.

Without Casey helping me to see that I was speaking sarcastically about him, I would not have realized the negative impact it would have had on our relationship. I said, "I don't know how to change that."

He replied, "Well, if you have something to say to me, let's learn how to have those conversations." Oh, my goodness! I didn't know how to walk down that renewal path. It was a whole new way of thinking for me.

When you have made the decision to renew the spirit of your mind, there will be things the Spirit of God brings to you that you don't understand at first. Take the time to listen when someone speaks into your life. You might feel embarrassed and uncomfortable at the time, but it will be so worth it!

One of our friends told us a story about their grandma. She was at a place in her life where she could not take care of her house anymore. She was really struggling. She couldn't take care of the yard or manage the cleaning and the maintenance that comes with owning your home. She was struggling with so many things but just didn't want to let go of her home. She didn't want help, and she certainly wasn't going to move. She was comfortable with the way things were, and she refused to change. She became angry at her family for trying to force her out of her comfort zone.

Do you know your *comfort zone* has nothing to do with what is best for you? It has nothing to do with what is right. It's just what you're comfortable with. Some people are comfortable with being abused. Others are comfortable with abusing themselves with their addiction, smoking habit, or bad eating habits. When we are comfortable and someone tries to make us change, we get angry. We all do it. We resist. We say, "Stop messing with me! I may not like my bad habit, but I'm not changing until I'm good and ready"—because we're comfortable.

When did we start calling it *comfort food?* What is comfort food anyway? Mashed potatoes...potato chips...a big bowl of chicken noodle soup? What is your go-to comfort food? Your favorite candy bar? A pint of ice cream? Maybe for you, it is a full southern meal of fried chicken, mashed potatoes and gravy, with biscuits and honey.

I suppose *comfort food* is whatever food comforts you. Does it have to be healthy? That would be no! No one has ever told me asparagus is their comfort food! Normally, comfort food is something not necessarily good for you, but it makes you *feel* good. You get the big bucket of fried chicken—and yum—eating it makes you feel so good. That's a good comfort food, right?! Throw in some biscuits and gravy, and it doesn't get any better than that. You know you might gain six pounds after eating that bucket of chicken, but you just can't resist. As you are eating it, you know that it doesn't supply what you truly need, but it's comfortable, so you eat it anyway.

Our strongholds are firmly rooted in what makes us feel comfortable. Even though we don't like our situation, we're comfortable with it, so we continue in the same old rut. Your stronghold is that comfortable thought; the one you hang on to like that old pair of slippers. You know it's not okay. You know it won't bring about your prosperous soul. Even though you know it's not right, you choose to be comfortable. You reject change due to the discomfort it will bring.

When I was first saved, I spent seven years going to the Monroe State Penitentiary in Washington State to minister to the inmates with Julius, my mentor. Every week, we sat in dirty, dark cells and talked to prisoners who were serving sentences anywhere from two to forty years and some for life. As a counseling team, Julius and I would discuss the men who were about to be released. We knew that statistically 80 percent of the inmates, if they were released, would be back. As we spoke with each man, we couldn't help wondering, *Is this one of those who will be back? Will this be one of the few who will change?* Do you know what the deciding factor was? Whether or not he was comfortable in prison. When an inmate was comfortable in prison, he would not be comfortable on the outside. In order to stay comfortable, he would rather be institutionalized.

Have you become *institutionalized* in your problem? Are you *institutionalized* in your negative situation? Have you become so comfortable with the thing you don't like, that you cannot be comfortable with the promises of God? That is why Paul told us in II Corinthians, chapter 10, "It's a stronghold! It's not easy to get rid of. You have to fight it." How do you do it? Pull down that stronghold by capturing every thought and bringing it into the obedience of Christ. Become *aware* of your thoughts, *focus* on the promises of God and *practice* your new thinking until it becomes routine.

Years ago we had a great friend who worked at a local restaurant on the south end of Seattle. She has since gone to be with the Lord, but she was such a good lady. She loved being a waitress, and we had many great conversations with her over the years. This woman had developed a hairstyle when she was in high school. It was perfect for her at that age and in that era. The funny thing was, she was in her forties when we met her, and we knew her until she was in her seventies, but not once did her hairstyle change. She was comfortable with that style, and in her mind any other style was wrong for her.

Can you imagine the dramatic impact it would have made on this lady's appearance if she had changed her hairstyle? But she never would. She wasn't open to change. She was a *get-in-a-rut-and-stay-there* kind of lady. She was never going to try a new cut, a new product, or a new way of styling her hair because it was outside her comfort zone.

We all know those people who just can't adjust to change. To them, it is practically sacrilegious to get rid of the old and try something new. They say things like, "I don't understand why we can't just do it the way we always have." They live for consistency, and for them it is nearly impossible to change.

Are you a person who is open to change? Can you see yourself living a renewed life? It won't be easy. It will be uncomfortable at first. You will start out feeling like you are not sure you can handle it. A new style always looks a little strange at first, doesn't it? A new way of doing things or a new outlook will always be a bit uncomfortable in the beginning. Once you begin to move forward, that is when you will start to get excited about the new things you are experiencing. God is new every day. When you are living like God, basing your life on His ways, you are not stuck in the old.

God is all about new things. God is the Creator of the new. From the beginning of the Bible to the end, God demonstrates His love for the new. A new day. A new morning. A new season. A new song. A new spirit. A new heart. He is looking forward to bringing forth a new people, a new Jerusalem, a new Heaven and a new Earth.

Lamentations 3:22-23 says that the mercy and compassion of God are new every morning. When you know this grace of God, you are able to embrace new things He does every day. You can keep those things that are foundational and good, yet still reach for the new. The world will try to keep you bound in your comfort zone, but grace will bring you to a new place—a place of change and renewal in the Lord. With His help. By His grace, the new things will soon feel right and you will be comfortable.

SIX

The Lies We Believe and the Truth that Sets Us Free

"Abide in my Word...and the truth will make you free."
—John 8:31-32

What is the one thing many teens and young adults do not want to hear? You are just like your dad!" "You remind me so much of your mom!" Although many of us—especially the younger we are—would disagree, we are much more like our parents than we care to admit. Most of us grew up with the same thoughts and beliefs as our parents—economically, spiritually, and relationally. In most cases, and unless something drastic happens, we end up living like our parents. We grow up with their thoughts and beliefs.

At some point in our young lives, many of us have to *sow our wild oats*. We have to rebel. It might not be as true in other countries, but especially in America, we've got to do our own thing. Although you may go *your* way for a while, eventually you will start sounding like your dad. You start looking like your dad. You start acting like your mom. You start living as you were raised. Some day you will look at your life, and you will say, "When did I become my parents?"

The Bible says in Proverbs 22:6, "Train up a child in the way he should go, And when he is old he will not depart from it." As young people, we may have experimented with choices that we were not raised to make. We might have run around, done the college party scene, and gotten an attitude; but in the end, how many of us have returned to the way we were raised? We end up sounding like our parents, acting like our parents, and living like our parents. Why? Because of the spirit of our minds.

You may have heard the story of the mom who was showing her daughter how to cook their traditional Christmas dinner. First, she got out the big, covered pan. Next, she got out all the ingredients: the ham and the yams, and all the things she would need for the side dishes. They were doing the whole deal—the big family dinner. Finally, the mom cut the ham in half and put it in the pan. The girl was curious, so she asked, "Mom, why did you cut the ham in half?"

The mom answered, "Well, that's the way we cook it."

The little girl asked, "Why do we do that, mom?"

The mom was stumped, so she said, "I don't really know. You should ask Grandma, because that's the way she taught me."

The little girl ran to the phone and called her grandma. She said, "Grandma, we're cooking Christmas dinner, and when we got to the ham, Mom cut the ham in half before she put it in the pan. I'm just wondering, why do you cut the ham in half?"

Her grandma said, "Well, I don't know why your mom cuts it in half, but I just never had a pan big enough for the whole thing!" Grandma had a practical reason for why she always cut the ham before she cooked it. Mom had a *spirit of the mind* reason. Grandma did it because she didn't have a pan big enough. Mom did it because that's the way she was raised. She didn't know why, but for her, it was *the way we do it*. It was part of her thinking.

What you teach your children is vital. You may not realize it, but your actions, your attitudes, and the way you live your daily life has an enormous impact on the future of your children. The choices you make in your life right now may be limiting the way your children will live as they grow and mature. You will stop them from realizing all God has for them when you tell them things like, "You can't. It won't work. We can't afford it. It'll never happen. We're not that kind of people. We've never had that before." When you put those thoughts into your child's mind, you may limit their destiny.

A Word from Wendy: Who Are You?

Who are the Treats? How do the Treats live? What do the Treats believe? These are a few of the questions we would ask our children as they were growing up. When one of our kids would say or do something that was not appropriate, we would ask, "Is that how a Treat would act?" In training them to think and act correctly, we would have a conversation and end with, "This is how the Treats live …. The Treats are very kind to people."

Why would we do this? We were developing godly qualities within them, which would, in turn, become *the spirit of their mind.* In helping to create the attitude that we wanted them to have, we would say things like, "Instead of honking at the car that is trying to pull in front of us, we are thoughtful to let them in." We would say, "When you are at school, and you have an issue with someone, don't get in their face and yell at them." I could tell you so many stories.

Our oldest son has a very strong personality. As parents, we encountered teachers and those in authority who always had certain labels they put on a strong kid. I have to say, there were are few times he was a little bit too tough on some kids in school, and Casey and I would say to him over and over, "That is not how we act. Treats speak kindly and help others." We would always give a biblical word along with what we were saying.

I hope you can see the picture I'm trying to create for you. It was important to train our kids—and in turn, fill the spirit of their minds— with the thought, "This is how the Treats live. The Treats live with kindness towards others. The Treats live generously and always care for other people." Did we always live up to that standard? No, because we are not perfect, but it was the goal. We didn't ignore what was wrong. When one of our children acted in an inappropriate way, it wasn't that we didn't see it or correct it, but by the end of the conversation we wanted to reinforce that the Treat's live a certain way.

By creating a way of living in the spirit of your mind, it helps you think about what you are doing and why. Instead of reacting with greed, you respond with generosity. That is *who* you are. You have created within the spirit of your mind a response that immediately takes the lead. In every situation, godly words, actions, and attitudes will come out of the abundance of who you are.

It's not hard to make sure that you are putting godly attitudes, biblical concepts, and scriptural thoughts into the hearts and minds of your children. How you talk to them, how you react to various situations, and how you respond to them is crucial. Of course, the number-one way that you train up your child is by your example. Contrary to what you might want to believe, it is not your words but your actions that matter most.

You can say all the right words, but if your actions do not line up with what you are saying, your children will rebel. If your example is shallow relationships, being unfaithful, and not being generous—mediocre Christianity—then the spirit of their minds becomes what you have modeled for them. Not only will they become mediocre Christians, but it's possible they may rebel against Christianity altogether.

I can't tell you how many Christians over the years have asked me why their children, who were raised in a Christian home, were not following God. Often it is because the right words were said, but the actions were never there. Our children are smart enough to realize when something is true in our lives or when we speak empty words.

Make sure you are the person you want your children to become.

A Word from Wendy: Don't Grow Weary

Moving again?! It was my senior year of high school, and my whole world was once again in turmoil. After much discussion, it was finally decided that my parents and younger siblings would move across the state, and I would move in with family friends whose children I had been babysitting. Unfortunately, the family was going through a disaster. The woman had just lost her father and her brother, both within the previous six months. Due to the consuming sense of sadness and depression within that family, I was basically on my own at age seventeen.

Although turmoil was all around me, I could feel the grace of God reaching out; and as He reached out to me, I reached back. I had grown up in church and attended service every week, but that did not mean I knew God. My parents had raised me in church, so I knew I needed to go to church to find what I was looking for.

I had no idea, the day I chose to attend a random church service, how much my life was about to change.. I don't remember much about the service, but I do remember feeling like God was speaking to me alone. Even in the midst of a huge crowd, I felt like it was just God and me. I knew right then that I needed to accept Jesus as my Lord and Savior. My parents had sown the Word into my heart for years, and I didn't need anyone to tell me what to do. I knew. I remember saying, "God I want this. I want to know You. I want to live for You." That was the moment I forever surrendered my life to God.

As I look back at my story—and as you look back on yours—it is easy to see how God has worked in our lives and that He will continue to work. It helps us look towards the future with hope when we understand how much God has done in our past.. When you realize the different moments of time—the ones no one saw and those you didn't even know were significant—you can clearly see the hand of God at work on your behalf.

How you were raised by your parents, the culture you were raised in, and the nation you live in are all contributing factors to the *spirit of your mind*. Look at the many different people groups—whether it is a country, an organization, or a church—and you will see every possible style of dress, behavior, likes, and dislikes. The way you are raised will manifest in the *spirit of your mind*. It will show up in the way you do business, in the way you approach your marriage, and in the way you raise your children.

Your concepts of right and wrong, good and evil, and what is acceptable or not acceptable, become a part of the spirit of your mind and come from your culture, the home you were raised in, or whatever culture you decide to embrace. How many of us ever stop to question our beliefs? Do you ask, "Is this good? Is this right? Is this God's way, or is it just my way?" When is the last time you questioned the way you live, the choices you make? Upon closer examination, you might be doing things that aren't necessarily God's way.

What's your favorite style of music? Why do you like that particular style of music? Is it classical or rock and roll? Why do you prefer rock and roll? If you like rap, why do you like rap? Is it possible that in your teenage years somebody you thought was cool liked it, so you liked it too? You liked them, and because of that you liked that style of music. Or maybe it was just normal for you in that season of your life.

Scientists say that at around fourteen years of age we begin to develop our musical tastes, and our preferences are pretty well set by the time we reach the age of twenty-four. Some people may change their preferences as years go by, but it is uncommon for any dramatic shifts to occur. You can learn to enjoy other styles, but generally speaking, what you liked when you were a teenager and into your college years is what you like today. That's why there are Oldies stations.

The other day someone asked me, "What music do you listen to most on your phone?" I wanted to be spiritual. I wanted to tell him, "Christian." I wanted to say Christian Faith Center worship music. I really wanted to be spiritual, but honestly, I don't listen to much music on my phone. To tell the truth, if I'm on an airplane, and I decide to listen to music, I turn on Lynyrd Skynyrd, ZZ Top, and a few other rock and roll bands. You know, the kind of music my kids have never heard of! The music that hasn't been around for forty years. The music that was cool when I was sixteen, and I had my eight-track tape blasting in my Mustang as I was rolling down the freeway on my way to jail.

At this point in my life, I spend more time listening to worship music; but the music I was drawn to as a teenager is what is on my phone. It's on my iTunes list, and if I could pick one thing to listen to in my spare time, it would be my old rock and roll music. Why do I still like that style of music? It is a part of the spirit of my mind.

Have you ever sat and just watched people? What they wear, how they walk, and how they act and interact with others? I find people-watching a fascinating way to pass the time. I read somewhere that there are over seven billion of us on the planet, and that number is increasing every second of every day. The amazing thing is, every single one of us is unique. Unless you are in jail or in some other restrictive situation, you choose each day how you will dress, what you want to eat, and where you work. Some of us like a casual dress style while others love to dress up. Some eat meat; some are vegetarians. No two people on the planet are identical. Even identical twins are not *identical*.

We also find uniqueness when looking at the many different cultures found around the world. One group of people loves tortillas and frijoles. Another group of people prefers Kimchi and octopus. Another group likes hot dogs and apple pie. Although all regions of the world have a certain sameness, there is diversity among the groups. There is a common thread, but no two people groups like exactly the same things, even two people within a particular culture can differ.

One thing that fascinates me is the question, *Why do we like what we like?* The simple answer is this: Each one of us has a part of our mind that automatically makes certain decisions for us. You don't sit down before eating a meal and ask yourself why you like a particular food; you just like it. You can't explain why you do; you just do. You wouldn't know how to explain why you can't stand something; you simply don't like it. Often, the thing you can't stand is the very thing that someone else loves. How you process your likes and dislikes are part of what makes you unique. It has to do with what you were exposed to or with the way you were raised. It has to do with your personality. It has to do with choices you've been making since you were young—over and over and over again.

What things are you doing and you don't know why you do them that way? How many things do you like, and yet you don't understand why you like them? How many attitudes or beliefs do you have, and yet you don't know why you have those beliefs? As you engage in the process of renewing your mind, I would ask you to explore and challenge yourself with these questions: Why you do the things you do, say the things you say, and think the things you think? You might be surprised with what you come up with.

Have you ever experienced a time when everything was just *too good?* You may not say, "Things are too good," but subconsciously you are thinking, *Uh-oh, things are going too good lately. There must be a disaster on the way. When things are going this good, I'm sure a problem is coming!*' Subconsciously you are waiting for *the other shoe to drop.* Why would you think that? The *spirit of your mind* is telling you that things should not be this good. It's abnormal. And, you don't know what to do when things are going *too good.* You need to return to a feeling of *normal;* which, for you, is dealing with an on-going relationship struggle, financial lack, or problems on the job.

When things are a little too good, we find a way to bring ourselves back into a place that feels familiar. I have heard of corporate studies where they have tested this theory. They take the salespeople from highly successful regions and those who are from the less successful areas and they switch them. The less successful person will always say things like, "There are no good customers here. I can't find the good clients. I don't get the chances the other guy gets. It's not fair. I can't make a living."

In the test, the less successful salespeople were given the area where others made the most money, and the successful salespeople went to those areas where, apparently, there were no good customers. Amazingly, in less than one year, the less successful salespeople had ruined the sales in the good district and lost a majority of the customers. On the other hand, in less than one year the successful salespeople had raised the sales in their region, acquired new clients, created new opportunities, and found a way to prosper.

In Matthew 12:35, Jesus said, "A good man out of the good treasure of his heart brings forth good things, and an evil man out of the evil treasure brings forth evil things." Don't sabotage the opportunities that God is placing before you. Success is often uncomfortable at first, and we tend to move unconsciously towards what makes us comfortable. Take care that you do not unwittingly ruin the good by doing something foolish to get back to *normal*—whatever that feels like to you.

How often do you unconsciously do the very thing that will bring back struggle into your life? It's because struggling feels normal. You get the bills paid off, and it feels so good—for a while. Within a few weeks, you use all the charge cards and find yourself right back where you were. Why? It feels normal for you to be in debt and barely able to get by. Whatever it takes, you put yourself right back in the position you worked so hard to get out of. Don't do that! Don't unconsciously do the thing that will bring you back to your normal level of comfort. Make a conscious decision and do whatever it takes to make your *new normal* feel comfortable.

Have you ever heard someone say, "Oh, that's just too nice. I could never drive a car like that. I could never afford a house like that. That's too much for me. I could never go to a church like that. It's way too big." These lies and other ungodly thoughts place unconscious limitations on your future growth and keep mediocrity ruling in your life. When these types of negative thoughts are controlling you, you limit what God can do in your life. You believe the lie.

You may believe the lie that convinces you that you need to stay at a certain economic level. In fact, you never go beyond the economic level of your parents. Again, it goes back to feeling comfortable. Do you only feel comfortable when your world is predictable and safe— when everything feels normal? Is it safer to believe the lie that *you can't do any better* than it is to believe God's Word that says, "Now to Him who is able to do exceedingly abundantly above all that we ask or think, according to the power that works in us..." (Ephesians 3:20)?

Another word I like to use for safe is *mediocre*. Don't get me wrong. There is a world of difference between responsible and mediocre. We all need to make wise choices and be responsible for paying our bills and taking care of our homes and families. What I'm talking about is a step below responsible, into a place that is mundane. It is that risk-free zone that feels safe, the place where we let safe become mediocre.

A few words that define *mediocre* are: ordinary, lackluster, forgettable, average, middle-of-the-road, uninspired, and unexceptional. I could go on, but I think you get the idea. Mediocre is easy. It is not hard to stay in your rut and just get by. You don't have to put out much effort to get by, and it is less stressful just to accept what is easily within your grasp.

How many of us settle for a mediocre, middle-of-the-road existence? You know, like the person who, when you ask how they are, responds, "I'm okay." You ask how they are doing and hear, "Better than nothing." They are either afraid of the risk or can't be bothered to seek for more. Not only are they living a mediocre life, but they also frown on those who want more. They argue about the scriptures that say God has something more for us. They fight against the truth of God's promises because it often feels like it is just too much. The risk is too great, and they can't see beyond their mediocrity.

How can you get rid of the lies and lift the limits in your life? You first have to recognize the lies you have believed and how those lies have set limits in your life, limits in your spiritual life, limits in your health, and limits in your relationships. How often have you thought, *I could never have that; it's too nice! I could never wear a coat like that; it's too expensive. I wish I could be healed, but it's never going to happen; it's too much to ask.* Why is it too much or too nice for you? Who told you it was too much? Where did you hear that lie?

Subconsciously, in the spirit of your mind, you have set certain levels of what you can expect in your life. You have a certain economic level, a type of car or home you can own, a type of clothing you can purchase. You may even have a certain level of spirituality you can attain, set by how you see your relationship with God.

Many think the pastors or priests have access to God that they will never have. They put a middle-man between themselves and the clergy because most people would never presume to ask God directly for anything. Religion has taught us for centuries that only the pastor can get God to hear and answer their prayers. This religious belief holds many in bondage and fear—and keeps them from knowing God personally.

Unless you change the way you think, you will set limits for every area of your life, and you will continue to live within those limits all of your life. When your mind accepts a level you are comfortable with, you will naturally gravitate towards anything equal to or below that level. You unconsciously create situations that will keep you from rising higher than your established belief. What would happen if you could raise your beliefs—and the level of your life? What if you lifted your vision to see that you could have something better, something higher?

God is not holding you back from success in life. He wants you to be healed, to have a great marriage, and to experience success in every realm of life. Remove the lies that limit you and believe there is more for you in life. Why not you? Why not start now?

SEVEN

Loving Yourself While Pursuing Change

Love God, love people, LOVE YOURSELF.
—based on Matthew 22:37-39

Have you ever met a person who thinks God is mad at them or disappointed with them? You might be surprised how many people grow up thinking that very thing. You might even be one of those people. One who has thoughts like, *I've failed the Lord. I've done too much! I turned my back on God. Why would He want me now?* If you grew up with a church background and then walked away, you probably feel guilty when you think about the Lord. If you grew up in a denominational church, you probably feel like God is disgusted with you because of the choices you have made. If someone asked, "What does the Lord think of you? Your response might be; "I'm not sure." The fact is—He loves you. He's for you. He wants you to experience His plan, and His plan and purpose for you is good.

The devil wants you to think God is mad at you. What better way to keep you from living the powerful life you were created to live than to put a barrier between you and God. If he can keep you ashamed or embarrassed or hurt, you will never tap into the goodness of God. That is why you must capture every thought that moves you away from God—fear, anger, unforgiveness—every unscriptural thought!

A Word from Wendy: God's Amazing Grace

The first time I stole was at age four. Being a pastor's kid, my family moved every few years, and being the *new kid*, I needed some candy to give to my new little friend. Since I didn't have any money, I stole the candy. When our family moved to another location, I again stole a little jewelry set, and I gave it to my newest little friend. Why did I steal? I needed something to give them so that they would like me.

As I look back at that part of my history, I realize that I was trying to buy my way in—into my friendships, into love and affection, and into acceptance. There was something in me that made me feel that, by myself, I didn't have anything of value to offer. I was not shy or weak, but I still had a feeling inside that made me need to have more to give than just *who I was*.

As I look back, I can see how overwhelmed I was with inferior thoughts of, *I'm not good enough; You won't like me—who I really am—so I have to give you something. I have to find a way into your heart.* Even though I was raised in a pastor's home and was in church every week, I continued to steal throughout my growing up years. I didn't stop until I got saved, which was at age seventeen. Not only is that a lot of stealing, but also it is a lot of years of building upon the idea that I needed to buy my friendships.

When I got saved, God immediately touched me in the depth of my soul and helped me recognize that I did not need to pay to be accepted. He had already paid it all. When I look back at that moment in time, I am so grateful. I had tried to earn love and affection all my life. I attempted to fit in by giving away things, and yet God already accepted me! He gave me the greatest gift—complete love and acceptance.

A critical key to renewing your mind is becoming free from your past. John 20:23 says, "If you forgive the sins of any, they are forgiven them; if you retain the sins of any, they are retained." God wants you to live with a spirit of forgiveness. Forgiveness is the key to change. Freedom comes when you forgive, and it is a vital part of your process of renewal. For many people, it is not easy to forgive; in fact, it can be downright messy and painful and hard. You won't experience the growth you desire until you allow the hurts of the past to be released from your life.

We all have issues we need to deal with. Some issues are personal; some have to do with others. We have habits and behaviors we need to overcome, and to get anywhere in the renewal process, you must first forgive yourself. If you think God is mad at you, or you are mad at yourself for choices in your past, you will never move on from those mistakes. Mark 11:25 says, "And whenever you stand praying, if you have anything against anyone, forgive him, that your Father in heaven may also forgive you your trespasses." To pursue the change you want in your life, you must forgive—*others, yourself, and you may even feel you need to forgive God.* Forgiveness does not mean another person, or God for that matter, has done anything wrong. The act of forgiveness often helps us come to terms with feelings of betrayal or bitterness. Forgiveness does not mean you forget or instantly feel better. It just means you choose to move forward. You let go of the negative emotions and try to move on.

A Word from Wendy: Don't Give Up—On Yourself or Others

We were in California one summer, and my mom was driving us to an event. I had one of my good friends with me, and my mom was giving a ride to a man who was part of the event. I didn't know him, but at one point he turned around, looked at me, and said, "Hey, Wendy, how's your relationship with Jesus?" I was in the 8th grade and full of rebellion—especially towards my mom. Well, I figured that my mom had put him up to it, right? I was so mean-spirited that I looked at him and growled, "Don't talk to me!" Then I said, "If you want to talk in this car, talk to my friend!" and I pointed to my friend who was sitting next to me. I was just mean.

All I can say is that I am so grateful God sees beyond those moments, and so thankful that my mom—even as mean as I was—prayed for me. I know that I hurt her feelings over and over. My mom could have been so humiliated and looked at that moment and said, "Oh my goodness, Wendy's going to Hell." I actually *was* at that point.

God used that moment in my life—and He has used those same moments when you too have been at your worst—to speak something into your heart. I watched that man as he ignored my meanness, turned to my friend, and talked about the love of God. As he spoke, some of those words penetrated my heart also. I was sitting in the car, as mean-spirited as a snake, and was still touched by the love of God.

Years later I asked my mom, "Who was that guy in the car?" She told his name and then she said, "Actually, he is at a local church right now, so why don't you see him?" I said, "Done!" I went to the church and found that man. I looked at him in the face and said, "Thank you." I thanked him because he did not let my ugliness stop him from sharing the goodness and love of God.

God saw me. God sees you. Even during the worst moments of your life—when you were the meanest, when you did things that you were ashamed of—God still saw you. He was reaching out to you with His grace and love because that's what God does.

Second Corinthians 4:16 tells us, "Therefore we do not lose heart. Even though our outward man is perishing, yet the inward man is being renewed day by day." God doesn't want us to lose heart or become discouraged over our failures. He does not hold those things against us and does not want us to hold them against ourselves. Continue to work on the things that need to change in your life, and do not become disheartened when you miss the mark. More than anything else, He cares about your heart. Matthew 15:18-20 tells us, "Those things which proceed out of the mouth come from the heart, and they defile a man. For out of the heart proceed evil thoughts.... These are the things which defile a man."

In teaching the disciples, the Lord is saying, "Stop worrying about all the rules and regulations. Stop worrying about all the things on the outside. How you wash your hands means nothing to God. He is not concerned about that. The Lord doesn't care about the small stuff...He cares about your heart."

We love to create traditions. Often the rules and judgments we base our lives on are man-made and have nothing to do with the inner person. These things have nothing to do with your walk with God or what He wants to do in your heart. God deals with your heart and with the hearts of all humanity. He is not looking at the condition of the Moon, or how the stars are lining up. He doesn't care about your astrology chart or observing certain festival days or bowing three times while saying a specific chant. These types of rituals are merely distractions, causing you to forget that life comes out of your heart.

Out of your heart comes your growing family, your prosperity, and your spiritual life. Out of your heart comes your godly marriage and successful relationships. Jesus told us that *the things that go into your mouth are nothing. That which comes out of the heart is what matters.* It is interesting that the first thing Jesus lists in Matthew 15:19 is regarding your thoughts. He said, "For out of the heart proceed evil thoughts." Due to the context of the writing, Jesus specified evil thoughts, but we need to realize that our good thoughts also come out of the heart. Out of the heart—the spirit of your mind—come your thoughts. And, whatever comes from your heart controls your life.

Romans 5:8 tells us, "But God demonstrates His love towards us, in that while we were still sinners, Christ died for us." As Christians, one of the hardest things to renew our minds to is understanding and accepting the love of God. It's hard to grasp how much God loves us—that He loved us when we were at our worst—and loves us still. He saved us while we were at our worst. He died for us when we were undeserving and ungrateful. He continues to love and forgive us now, in spite of our imperfections, our failures, and our unbelief.

On your worst day, God loves you.

I want to say it again: God isn't mad at you. He accepts you as you are. You can't try to get Him to accept you; He already does. God doesn't have any rules about how you must behave for Him to love you. He just does. You can't do enough to earn God's love or acceptance. Too often, we work at trying to change and get ourselves together, but God isn't asking that of us. He has already forgiven every sin, every mistake, and every broken promise. Everything you see as sinful or bad—Christ has already forgiven. God so loved the world (even you) that He gave His only Son for you and me (John 3:16).

The sad thing is, we often hold our past against ourselves or others. We try to change ourselves, working to overcome the problems of our past on our own. It never works. There isn't anything you can do to change your past or rewrite your story. He doesn't ask you to. Thank God that once you were born again He erased your past. You are forgiven, and your past is forgotten.

Psalm 103:12 says, "As far as the east is from the west, So far has He removed our transgressions from us." It's not always easy, this walk with Christ. As you continue to walk in the grace God has given you; keep yourself grounded in His love and forgiveness. Don't think that God is mad at you. He loves you and wants you to succeed. He is for you. I can't say it enough, "If God is for us, who can be against us" (Romans 8:31).

EIGHT

Choices and Emotions

I set before you life and death, blessing and curse.

Therefore CHOOSE LIFE!

—Deuteronomy 30:19

Our emotions are a God-given gift, but God never designed our emotions to run our lives. Emotions are too volatile. They change far too quickly. One minute your emotions are up, and next they are down; they flip back and forth and end up somewhere in the middle. The key to your emotions is this: *They are never to be in charge.*

Your emotions follow what you think, what you believe, and what you choose. Unfortunately, we live in a society where we like to say, "I'm going to do what I feel is right." What does that mean? Where do you feel that? We make decisions based on thoughts like, *Well, you know, I just feel it is right for me. I've got to be me. I'm tired of other people telling me what to do. I've got to follow my feelings.* So what you are telling me is: *Your feelings are making your decisions.* All I can say to that is: *You're in trouble.*

How many marriages have failed because somebody felt like having an affair? How many kids don't have a dad because someone felt like moving on? How many wrong decisions are made because we have followed our emotions? You don't know how often I have felt like quitting. You don't know how many times I felt like not doing the right thing. We all have those feelings — almost every day! Having those feelings and acting on them are two different things.

A Word from Wendy: Emotional Blind Spots

We are so comfortable with our depression. We are so comfortable with a victim mentality. We become comfortable with our anger, comfortable with our sarcasm, and comfortable with our sadness. I have talked to people who had a sad situation happen in their life, and as they tell the story, I feel so sorry for them. Then I ask, when did this happen? They say it was twenty years ago. They are still wrapped up in the depths of despair over it and have become involved with the spirit of depression and grief. It's so easy to get comfortable with grief and begin to see everything through the eyes of your pain.

Just as I grew up with and was comfortable being sarcastic, it is much more satisfying when I am kind. In reality, there is no good feeling in your soul when you are involved with negative emotions. Those emotions bring about darkness, despair, and discouragement in your life, and there is absolutely no benefit to having them.

God wants us to get on a pathway of joy. He wants us to walk on the path of living in peace. He wants us to begin overcoming the issues in our lives. Instead, our blind spots often stop us from seeing what is happening on the inside. Sarcasm was astronomical in my life. Talking negatively was as normal to me as breathing, but I had to make a choice: Did I want to stay comfortable or did I want to reach for the ways of God? We all have a choice to make.

Don't follow your feelings. Follow what you *know* is right and what you've *chosen* as right, and then your emotions will follow your decision. How often do you start out doing the right thing, with no emotion at all, or sometimes even with a negative emotion? You think, *I'm doing what's right, but I'm not having any fun.* Or you think, *I'm doing what I know is the good thing to do, but it doesn't feel all that good.* After the fact is when you will usually start feeling good about it. Then you think, *Oh man, I'm glad I did that.*

I can't tell you how many times I have started praying without a good feeling. I didn't feel the *prayer anointing* at 6:00 am as I rolled out of bed. I prayed because it was the right thing to do. If you asked me, "Do you feel like praying?" my response would be, "No, I feel like going back to bed!" But I prayed anyway...and I read my Bible...and I got up in the morning to spend time seeking God because my soul doesn't follow my flesh or my emotions; my soul follows my spirit.

God made us a three-part being. We are made up of our spirit, our soul, and our body. Our soul is the controlling factor between our spirit and our flesh. To be *spiritually minded* means your soul is following your spirit. To be *carnally minded* means your soul is following your flesh. When you let your mind be negative or selfish, when you allow emotions to rule, you are carnally minded. Your soul is the deciding factor in the equation.

Our *soul* is another of those areas where we often make up our own definitions. But, if you want to know the truth, you have to go to the source of all truth—the Bible. The Bible has much to say about the soul.

"Jesus said to him, 'You shall love the Lord your God with all your heart, with all your soul, and with all your mind'" (Matthew 22:37). Hebrews 4:12 tells us, "For the word of God is living and powerful, and sharper than any two-edged sword, piercing even to the division of soul and spirit, and of joints and marrow, and is a discerner of the thoughts and intents of the heart."

The Bible also says, "For to be carnally minded is death, but to be spiritually minded is life and peace" (Romans 8:6). These verses tell us we have a choice. Will your soul agree with your spirit so that you will have life and peace? Or will your soul follow your body by making the carnal choices that ultimately bring death? When your soul follows your spirit, you will prosper in all things. When your soul follows your flesh, you will continually struggle with the strongholds that run your life.

Ask yourself, "Why didn't I get up this morning and read my Bible or pray?" If your answer is, "I didn't feel like it," I would say you are letting your fleshly emotions run your life. You are being *carnally minded*. It may feel comfortable for a time, but you will end up with results you don't want. Sleeping in feels good at the time. Eating the extra helping of fries tastes good for a little while, but the flesh is never satisfied, and it never satisfies you.

Just recently, it was 6:00 am and I was thinking, *Oh man, it's Saturday morning, and I should sleep in*. I didn't feel like getting up, but I've created a habit of being disciplined. I don't follow my feelings; my feelings follow me. My mind and my will are submitted to my spirit, right? So, I get out of bed. I make the bed. Get the sweats on. Start drinking my water. Have some protein. Drink my coffee and think to myself, *How am I feeling?* My response: *I feel tired. I feel slow. I feel groggy. I feel like I should have slept in.*

A few minutes later my daughter, Tasha, calls on the phone and says, "Dad, what are you doing?" I'm thinking, *It's 6:00 am! What do you think I'm doing? I'm just trying to survive!* I didn't say that, but I thought it! She knows Wendy is speaking out of town, so she says, "Do you want to run the stairs?" We have a great place to run up and down stairs near our home, which we regularly use for exercise. So I said, "Yeah, let's run the stairs." If she had said, "Do you feel like running stairs?" I would have said, "No!" But who cares what I feel like doing!

I'm sixty years old. I don't have time to worry about how I feel. Soon we're outside running stairs, checking the heart rate, running more stairs, again checking the heart rate, and running more stairs. Finally, we get back to the house, and suddenly I think to myself, *I'm feeling good!*

You know what would have happened if I had just rolled over and slept in? It would have been nine o'clock before I would have rolled out of bed. My sleep-fogged brain would be thinking, *What day is it?* When you follow your flesh, you often feel worse. But when you follow your spirit and do what's right, what's good, and what's godly, it feels good.

In Philippians 2:13, the *Amplified Bible* says, "For it is [not your strength, but it is] God who is effectively at work in you, both to will and to work [that is, strengthening, energizing, and creating in you the longing and the ability to fulfill your purpose] for His good pleasure."

God is energizing you, creating in you the longing and ability to fulfill your purpose. I love it! I wake up every day believing God is energizing me, creating the power in me that I need to do His will. I don't need to ask myself, "How do I feel?" I'll probably get the wrong answer. Do I feel like praying? Do I feel like studying? Do I feel like exercising? Do I feel like eating vegetables? I usually don't feel like it, so I don't ask myself.

Smith Wigglesworth, an evangelist who saw many miracles, said years ago, "What I feel is irrelevant. It's what I believe that matters." That's a good concept for us to catch hold of. How you feel is irrelevant. What you believe—that's what matters.

Don't ask how you feel; ask yourself what you *believe*. Ask yourself what you think according to Scripture. What do you believe God's plan is for your life? God is energizing, creating in you the power and the desire to do His will. Stop defining your life by your negative emotions, but rather be defined by the energy of God in your soul.

That is when you will find God's will.

"For those who live according to the flesh set their minds on the things of the flesh, but those who live according to the Spirit, the things of the Spirit. For to be carnally minded is death, but to be spiritually minded is life and peace. Because the carnal mind is enmity against God" (Romans 8:5-7).

Looking back at my own life, the times I felt the worst and struggled with my flesh the most, I was thinking in a very negative way. My own thoughts were setting me up for disaster. When I kept my head up, and my thoughts were in line with the thoughts of God, I could keep negative desires in check and live joyfully in God's will.

This passage from the book of Romans is talking to Christians. The apostle Paul is not talking to the world when he says, "You've got to have a spiritual mind if you want life and peace from God." As a Christian, you have a choice: You can have life and peace, or you can have a carnal mind. You can choose to follow your flesh, agreeing with the carnal mind, or you can fix your mind on the things of God. The saddest reality to me is this: You can be fully saved, loving the Lord, on your way to Heaven, but live a worldly, defeated life because you are following your flesh. We see it all the time.

A Word from Wendy: His Word is New Every Day

God is the same yesterday, today, and tomorrow; and yet, His Word and His ways are new every day. It sounds like a contradiction. The Scriptures tell you that God will always remain the same; yet, as He reveals His Word to you each day, you are given the ability to see it through fresh eyes. That is God's grace and the Holy Spirit continuously working in your life. That is the Spirit of God moving you towards His will day by day. His Word is new every morning. You don't renew in a day, or a month, or a year. Your Christian walk is an ongoing process from the day you get saved until the day you walk into Heaven.

When you follow your flesh, you think about the desires of your flesh. When you are following the things of the flesh, you are thinking about your next meal. You are thinking about that next thing you want to buy. You are thinking about drinking with the guys. You are thinking about partying and seeing who you might pick up at the bar. You are thinking about your fleshly desires. You are thinking about all the things that are not godly.

To live in the flesh means that your natural desires, such as laziness or selfishness, control your life. To live in the spirit means you are led by the Holy Spirit and the desires that come from your walk with God control your life. If you are like me, you have personally experienced both living in the flesh and walking in the spirit—sometimes even on the same day! One moment you are spiritual and thinking about how you can be a blessing to someone else, and the next moment you're angry or depressed and only thinking about yourself. How can you experience both behaviors in your life? The answer is simple: Your behavior is directly linked to whatever you are focusing on.

Romans 8:6 starts with, "For to be carnally minded is death." Death in this context means *to be separated from God*. He is not talking about physical death, but rather the death that comes from being disconnected or separated from God. The carnal mind brings death. It will keep you disconnected from the blessing of God, from the life of God, and from the favor of God.

Think about it this way: When a marriage is over, the husband and wife become separated. They are no longer one. Everything that had joined them together now becomes separate: their living arrangements, finances, hopes, and dreams. Death has come into the marriage relationship. They both still exist and go on with their lives, but the marriage is dead. There is no longer any meaningful connection. Many Christians are going on with life, but they are disconnected from the blessing of God. When we allow the carnal mind to dominate our lives, we become separate from the things of God.

Have you ever met a person and thought, "They seem so angry?" You feel uncomfortable or unsettled whenever you interact with them. You sense a change in the atmosphere whenever they come into a room. Hebrews 12:15 says, "...lest any root of bitterness springing up cause trouble, and by this many become defiled." That person most likely deals with a root of bitterness. Although you may not know why you feel uncomfortable with them, it has to do with the spirit of their mind.

A *bitter root* is often referred to in Hebrew culture as a plant with a poisonous root. It looks like a normal plant. You most likely won't see any difference on the surface, but underneath is something harmful, potentially painful, often deadly. Bitterness can also be called anger, unforgiveness, resentment, animosity, or hostility. Left to grow, it becomes the poison that will destroy your life.

Just as with a plant, the bitter root grows beneath the surface; so too, the bitterness in your life often lives below the surface of your mind. It exists without conscious thought on your part. As you walk through your day, you don't often consciously think about the people and situations that have hurt you or caused you pain. Most of us don't think about the hurts and emotional pains from our past, but often we have a root of hurt, anger, and bitterness growing under the surface of our lives.

A root of bitterness, left untended, will eventually spring up and destroy your life. We have all seen it happen, haven't we? People who are just grouchy and sour. You have heard of those who live for years with anger and unforgiveness, and then one day they die of a heart attack. Some who end up living alone, without family and friends, have driven away every relationship. This is because they would not let go of bitterness. The spirit of their mind was angry and hurt.

Acts 8:23 says, "For I see that you are poisoned by bitterness and bound by iniquity." People who live with a root of bitterness can't figure out why they are sick, why they cannot overcome problems, or why they feel so drained all the time. They wonder where their passion for life has gone. They don't understand why people never have time for them and are always busy when they call. The root of bitterness is destroying their lives.

Just as the root of bitterness will destroy your life, so will any negative emotion that has been allowed to control your behavior. Those emotions, which live below the surface of your consciousness, affect the spirit of your mind. They influence every decision. They cause you to say and do things you don't want to say and do.

The root of bitterness or anger is just one of the emotions that binds us up. What about a root of fear, depression, or worry? How many deal with a spirit of fear that is completely disabling? They become so bound up with fear and anxiety that they can no longer function normally. They cannot leave their homes, keep a job, or attend family functions. They are missing out on all life has to offer because a deep-seeded root of fear has taken over their emotions. Fear of people or flying or driving is often part of the roots in our mind—the spirit of the mind.

In our world today, allowing anger, strife, and fighting to control our thoughts and actions has become a new norm. Think about it. Many are fighting racial fights. social fights, national and international fights. We are fighting in the Middle East, fighting in Africa, and fighting terrorism around the world. Why is there this constant fight going on? Because there is no peace. You might think, *Well, of course, we are fighting because there is no peace.* No, it is because there is *no peace* that we are fighting.

Anger toward others comes out of a heart of *no peace*. Sadly, our TV shows and media love a good fight. How many shows are based on fighting and squabbling? You've got everything from *Divorce Court* to *Jerry Springer* to the unhappy *Housewives*—and they are welcomed into your living room every night of the week. How can we deal with road rage and blatant anger in a godly way when hostility is modeled as an acceptable method of communication?

Racism comes from a heart of *no peace*. Fighting amongst tribes and nations comes out of people who have *no peace*. Depression is the result of a life with *no peace*. Drug and alcohol use—the type used to manage your emotions and help you try to feel better—comes from a heart with *no peace*.

Sadly, drugs and alcohol will never bring true inner peace. A life with *no peace* is often found surrounded by the outer *things* that bring a sense of false peace. Extravagant materialism, substance abuse, or a daily quest for something to make us feel better is often the result of a lack of peace.

As I was walking in downtown Seattle recently, I realized, *Maybe I've been a Christian too long. I've been saved for so long that I don't even know what's going on in the world.* As I was walking, I noticed that people were smoking pot on the sidewalk. Someone said to me, "Hey, you want to buy some pot?"

I said, "Uh, I'm a pastor."

He asked again, "You want to buy some pot?

I laughed and answered, "No thanks." I've been there and done that! I have something better. I don't need to buy it, don't need to smoke it, don't need to eat it. I've found something better. If you have no peace, you will try to buy something, smoke something, or drink something that will help you feel good for a while.

How often do we try to fill our need for peace with a new relationship, a hobby, or even a new career? We bypass the need for the peace of God—a need that is crying out in our heart—with a natural answer. We try to replace our spiritual need with fleshly satisfaction. And still, as hard as we try, we find *no peace.*

Isaiah 26:3 says, "You will keep him in perfect peace, Whose mind is stayed on You, Because he trusts in You." I love this verse, *He will keep us at peace when our mind is right with Him.* The spiritual mind is filled with life and peace. You don't need to medicate yourself when you have the mind of Christ. The apostle Paul wrote, "Be anxious for nothing, but in everything by prayer and supplication, with thanksgiving, let your requests be made known to God; and the peace of God, which surpasses all understanding, will guard your hearts and minds through Christ Jesus" (Philippians 4:6-7).

If you can get your mind and emotions to submit to your spirit, you will live in the peace of God. How would it change your world if you could actually know the peace of God? I'm not saying it will be quick or easy. Nothing worthwhile happens overnight. But, if you can change one thought, you'll forever change your life.

When you keep your mind stayed, fixed, and focused on Him, you will live in perfect peace. Don't let that old spirit of your mind rise up. Don't allow the old way, the cultural way, the *way we've always done it* to control you. To live by your emotions means that your fleshly desires control your life. To live in the spirit means the peace of God controls your life.

Allowing your mind to focus on the things of the flesh will always bring worldly, negative behavior. Your emotions will be out of control because you will do whatever you *feel* like doing. When you set your mind on the things of the spirit, you rise to a higher level of life. You do the things that cause your walk with God to flourish, and you are a blessing to those around you.

Looking at my own life, when I feel the worst and struggle with my flesh the most, I am thinking the wrong thoughts. My own thoughts are setting me up for a disaster. When I keep my head up, and my thoughts are in line with the thoughts of God, I keep harmful desires in check and live with the peace and blessing of God.

The change you desire in the way you feel starts in your mind. If you can focus your thoughts on the thoughts of God, you'll begin to sense the peace of God. As His peace guards your heart and your mind, you won't need the drink, the joint, or the tranquilizer to find peace. Even much of our TV viewing or sports watching is just an attempt to ignore the reality of our lives. You go to the game so you don't have to think about the issues on your job, in your marriage, or with your finances.

Think of the all the things you do because you are nervous, frustrated, stressed, or depressed. What do you do when those negative emotions begin to take control of your mind? Do you start looking for ways to medicate your discomfort? If you could make changes in those areas of your life and have peace about them, you wouldn't need the distraction the world is offering you every day. You wouldn't need the beer to get away from your normal feelings, and you wouldn't need the pain killer to deal with the pain of your reality.

Jesus is called the *Prince of Peace,* and the Holy Spirit leads us by the *peace of God in our hearts.* If you are in turmoil, confusion, and frustration all the time, it's impossible to sense the peace of God. You start looking for peace replacements and pseudo supplements to fill the void. You medicate your pain with a boyfriend you don't really like, comfort food you shouldn't eat, or hours of TV you shouldn't watch. The next thing you know, you're drinking too much and finding yourself with health or career problems—all because you don't have the peace of God to guard your heart.

God's peace is real. It is available to all who seek it, and it will make a practical difference in your everyday life. The person who is angry in their car on the freeway, the guy at work who is always grumpy, the neighbor who is too sad to get out of their pajamas and come outside, or the business person who thinks the next million dollars will make them happy, are all looking for peace. The things they do are not working. After forty, fifty, or sixty years of that kind of living, they will be burned out, stressed out, or addicted to something. God has a better plan!

As you continue on your journey of renewal, become aware of the things you do to either find peace in your life or avoid the pain you feel. What are some of the thoughts that create turmoil in your life? As you focus your thoughts on the promises of God and begin to feel the peace of God, all those other things will become less and less important. You won't need to avoid your reality because it is not so bad. The changes in your thoughts will become the lifestyle changes you will see on your job, in your relationships, and throughout your day. The life and peace of God is a wonderful thing!

NINE

If You Think You Can—or—if You Think You Can't

For as he thinks in his heart, so is he.
—Proverbs 23:7

If you think you can—you can. If you think you can't—you can't. It's pretty simple. If, in the depths of your heart, you think you *can* do something, you're right. If you honestly think you *can't* do it, you are also going to be right. This is because your thoughts become your beliefs, and your beliefs create your lifestyle. Do you think you can grow, prosper, and have peace? Do you believe you can have joy, find love, and enjoy lasting friendships? Do you really believe that you can? Then, you can.

If you let it happen, society, public school, and the media will fill your mind with negative thoughts. The world, unhindered and unfiltered, will fill your mind with wrong thinking. By age nineteen, my mind was taking me down a dark and destructive pathway. I saw myself stuck in a dark hole and could not see any way out. At one point, I remember my mom putting me on suicide watch. That's how seriously concerned she was. I had no hope. I just wanted to die. I could not see any other way out of what my life had become.

The Bible teaches us in Proverbs 13:12, "Hope deferred makes the heart sick," and in Proverbs 29:18, "Where there is no revelation, people cast off restraint." When we don't see a way out of our problems, we become sick and hopeless, and we "cast off restraint." We don't even try anymore. We don't care if we hurt ourselves, because we can't see a light at the end of the tunnel. I was at the point where I thought I was stuck forever in my negative life, and there was no hope of escape.

I think there are so many who can relate to my story. Maybe you are stuck in a negative job or feel trapped in a bad relationship. You might be bogged down in a tremendous amount of financial debt, and you just can't see any way out from under the pressure. I was stuck in a life of negative friends, divorced parents, and low self-worth. My answer was to medicate the pain. My answer was, "Let's avoid reality. The less time I have to be awake, the less time I have to think about all the negatives in life."

Maybe you are like I was. That person who is trying to medicate the pain of your reality. Unfortunately, everything I did only caused more problems—a string of DUI's, in and out of jail, probation—and it just kept on getting worse. I was stuck in a life that was spinning from bad to worse.

One day my dad dropped me off at a house at 421 Jackson Street, in Seattle, WA. It was an old house, and is now an historical monument, with a nice plaque on the front door. In 1974 it had been turned into a drug rehab center. I'll never forget the first time I walked up those front steps. On the other side of the front door was the man who would change my life forever.

Have you ever been in the place where it's so dark that there's just nothing you can look forward to, the place where there is no light at the end of the tunnel? That's where I was the day I walked into the Washington Drug Rehabilitation Center. My worst day was the beginning of my best days.

That day, Julius said to me, "Big Red, you can change." Julius Young was the founder and director of WDRC. At that moment, I believed with all my heart I was stuck in the life I had created: I couldn't get healthy, I couldn't be strong, I couldn't overcome my addictions, and I couldn't get off probation. No matter how hard I tried, I could not get out of the cycle of destruction I was in. I couldn't get a job, I couldn't get ahead, and I couldn't win.

I didn't believe I could do it, but when Julius said those words to me, I believed *him*. I thought, *Well, maybe he has a secret potion, or maybe he's going to get me tapped into something.* I didn't believe I could do anything, but I did believe in him. You know the feeling. You come to church, and you're so stressed out, but you believe something that the preacher says, and you get a glimmer of hope. That is your beginning. One thought started something new in your life, just like one thought changed my life that day.

I had been arrested so many times, I would wake up in jail and have to ask somebody, "Why am I here?" I keep telling you my story because I want you to realize that your marriage can change, your health can change, and your finances can change. If I can change from the guy with no hope and nothing going for him and become who I am today—all because of one thought—you can change too.

Most of us have several, *I can't* thoughts. *I can't get to church on time. I can't keep up with everything going on in my family. I can't get out of debt. I can't lose weight. I can't....* What if we could just reach into your brain and pull out all the negative thinking.

Wouldn't that be awesome? Since *brain renewal surgery* is impossible, how else are you going to get rid of all those *I can't* thoughts?

Saying, "I can't," is often just an excuse. How many of us used to say, "I can't because I'm too young?" Now we say, "I can't because I'm too old!" Funny how that works. It doesn't really matter what your age is; it is your way of thinking that continually limits you from accomplishing all you could. You allow all your excuses about your age, your gender, or your nationality to take you out of the running.

What about the thought, *I can't because I don't have time? I don't have time to exercise. I don't have time to pray. I don't have time to read my Bible. I don't have time to talk with my family. I don't have time to....* That thought is a lie. You have the same amount of time that everyone else does. It's about how you're using the time you have. Examine how you spend the time you now have, and then challenge yourself to make any needed adjustments.

How about the thought, *I don't feel like it? I don't feel like eating healthy. I don't feel like going to church. I don't feel like serving. I don't feel like going to the gym.* What about *fear? I'm so afraid of what is happening with the economy. I don't know if I should travel with the way things are going. I just don't know if my kids are going to succeed.* You have to get those fearful thoughts out of your mind. The Bible tells us, "For God has not given us a spirit of fear, but of power and of love and of a sound mind" (II Timothy 1:7). Don't let fear control your mind.

What about *anger*? Have you said things like, "I'm so mad that I could scream," "I'm just so angry that I could spit," and "I feel so hurt that I may never get over it"? Every negative emotion comes from a host of negative thoughts. What if we could just reach in and pull those thoughts out? Would you do it if you could? I think you would. But it's not easy, is it?

In the book of Deuteronomy, God says that He sets before us life and death, blessing and cursing; and He strongly recommends that we choose life (Deuteronomy 30:19). He has always given us the choice—to choose His ways or the world's ways. He is telling you that in order to get rid of those negative thoughts, you have to make a conscious effort. You have to choose.

You have to decide, *I'm not going to think about that fear. I'm not going down that angry path in my mind. I'm not going to keep thinking bitter thoughts.* You have the ability to determine, *I'm not going down that path of thinking that I don't have the time, or I don't feel like it.* You have the choice to keep that thought out of your mind.

God has given you the ability to demand of yourself, *I'm not going there in my mind.* It's not a weekly, monthly, or yearly event, but a daily discipline. If you really think about it, you already know how to do it. You have already done it at some point. Think for a moment about what thoughts you have already taken authority over. It was and still is your decision to make. No one else can do it for you—it's *your* choice.

The way you take control of negative thoughts is to choose to replace them with God's thoughts. For instance, when you feel angry about a situation, put in thoughts about *forgiveness*. How do you *put* thoughts of forgiveness in your mind? You do what the Bible says. Luke 11:4 says, "Forgive us our sins, for we also forgive everyone who is indebted to us." As you meditate on these godly words, pray for forgiveness—for yourself and others —and then act on that forgiveness in your life. Renewal is replacing negative thoughts with God's—old thoughts with new.

Not only can you live with God's forgiveness of your sins, but you can renew your thinking to have forgiveness as a part of your future. You may ask, "Wait, you mean I can forgive before a problem even happens?" Yes, I believe you can. As you pray every morning, "Lord, forgive me, as I forgive those who sin against me," you forgive anything that might come up during the day that is ahead. You can have forgiveness on your mind before you even need it. You are creating a mindset of forgiveness. You are becoming a person who responds with forgiveness because that is part of who you are.

When somebody says to you, "I'm sorry I did that," your first response will be, "It's all right. I've already forgiven you." That's your mindset, your attitude, and that's the way you think. When your mind is renewed to God's way of thinking about forgiveness, you think *forgiveness*. You're not angry. You don't walk around mad all the time. You don't need to say, "You hurt my feelings," and then hang on to any negative feelings. You have *already* forgiven them. Rather than getting down and trying to get back up, let's learn to stay up. Keep your mind on Him.

What about taking your thoughts of fear and anxiety—all of your *I cant's*—and putting faith-filled thoughts into your mind instead? The Bible says, "But without faith it is impossible to please Him, for he who comes to God must believe that He is, and that He is a rewarder of those who diligently seek Him" (Hebrews 11:6).

Without faith it is impossible to please Him. Do you have faith on your mind? Are there faith-based thoughts filling your mind? What about thoughts of peace or the joy of the Lord? If you can say *yes*, then I would say you are on your way to a renewed mind.

What you fill your mind with on a daily basis will control your ability—and the level—to which you will be able to get rid of your negative thoughts. "A good man out of the good treasure of his heart brings forth good things, and an evil man out of the evil treasure brings forth evil things" (Matthew 12:35). As you store up the good treasure of God's Word in your heart and mind, you will bring forth those good things in your life.

A Word from Wendy: The Fear of Failure

As a young girl, everyone called me the *little momma*. I always loved babysitting and working with kids, so when Casey and I got married, of course, the first thing my family said was, "How soon are you going to have kids?" We were very involved with the drug rehab program where Casey had graduated, so most of our closest friends were graduates of the program.

Due to their history, our friends all had the perspective that it was not possible to raise kids who wouldn't end up getting arrested, taking drugs, and hurting people. As we began our marriage, the prevailing thought in my world was, *You should not have children!*

The people closest to you might be saying things like, "You can't start a business; it's way too risky." "You can't go to college; you could never pay for it, and you don't need that piece of paper anyway." "You should just marry him; who else is ever going to ask you?" As you settle for less than your heart desires, you are defeated before you begin.

Although the deepest desire of my heart was to have children, in this environment my vision of being a mom was being torn away conversation by conversation. I was told, "It is not possible to raise up godly children. They will just become drug addicts. They will not serve the Lord, and they will just hate you!" Without a doubt, my rebellion against my mom as a teen solidified my negative thinking.

Casey knew having kids was the dream of my future, so we would often talk about starting a family. We wondered if it would be possible for us to raise godly children. The devil had come to steal that dream, and so the answer was always, "Yeah, I don't think so."

One day I was devastated by a comment someone had made to me on another topic, and I did the only thing I knew to do. I went home and began to pray. Sometimes the only thing to do is to have a conversation with God. The answers you need won't come from reading a bunch of Twitter posts, looking on Instagram, or calling a friend.

As I prayed about this other situation, I did something that was very unusual for me. I asked God if there was anything I was not doing that He had planned for my future. I don't know why I even asked that question, but I did, and soon I heard Him say as loud as could be, "Have children."

I was shocked! Then I felt such peace. When Casey came home that night, I said, "Casey, I feel like God spoke to me about having children," and he looked at me and spoke what I believe was the Word of the Lord for us. He said, "I believe we're going to have two boys and a girl." Today we have two boys and a girl.

It would be great to say it was all easy after that. Overcoming something you believed you could never have is not easy. We had to find promises in God's Word as we renewed our minds for this new adventure. We had been married for seven years before having children, so the old thoughts did not just disappear. As we began looking to the Word and Spirit of God, we were given His wisdom and strength. For this new chapter in our lives to be successful, we knew we needed to be strong in Him. We began to take out the old, worldly thoughts and replaced them with God thoughts.

Our kids are adults now. They all love God. They didn't get into drugs. They were not perfect children, but they didn't do any of the things that I was so afraid they would do. They were normal kids.

They had normal issues, and they're now normal adults.

God possibly has something new in your future, but you've allowed your doubts and the *I cant's* to control your thinking until it has become a loud, booming voice in your head. I encourage you to quiet that loud, booming voice and just ask God, "Is there something in my life that I'm not doing today that you have planned for me?" It could be the beginning of the opportunity you have been dreaming about.

Intentionally sow positive, godly thoughts into your heart. Allow your mind to become filled with godly thoughts, scriptural thoughts, Holy Spirit thoughts; and always keep those God-breathed, lifegiving thoughts foremost in your mind. The truth of God's Word must be the foundation of your thought patterns. Your *go-to* thoughts must be based on truth not on how you feel or the circumstances around you.

Dream about what God has for you. Capture negative thoughts by visualizing all that God has for you. See yourself as the person you want to be. Instead of rehearsing what you don't want, think on what you do want. Believe you are positioned to receive God's best for this season of your life. You have a wonderful future ahead of you. God has so much more for you. As you put God's truth into your mind— think about and meditate on it—you will not only find the higher life you have been seeking, but also you will become the person you have always wanted to be.

TEN

Set Your Mind on Things Above

> Set your mind on things above,
> not on things on the earth.
> —Colossians 3:2

What does it mean to *seek* something? Remember when you couldn't find your car keys? The hunt is on. You're seeking them, right? It's that time you are trying to get ready to go, but you can't find your child because he took off with the neighbors' kids. You are seeking him. You want to wear your favorite blouse, but you can't remember if it's in the laundry, in the closet, or if one of your *favorite* children borrowed it. Now you are seeking it. You're focused, searching high and low for it.

These verses in Colossians are telling us, *If you are born again and if you are raised with Christ, you are to seek those things which are above*. What does it mean to seek the things of God? Pursue the things of God the way you pursue your car keys. Make the same effort with the things of God that you do when you turn the house inside out looking for that blouse. Do you pursue God with that same passion, or is your attitude, "If God wants me to have more, He'll just bring it to me"?

Sadly, I think most of us in the church are pretty laid back in our attitude toward the things of God. It's a kind of *hit and miss* approach. Generally speaking, in the church world the thought is, *Well, if God wants me to have it, He'll get it to me*. That's not the way it works. We are supposed to seek. Those who hunger and thirst will be filled.

Most men know how to seek. Isn't that true? For instance, you are excited about your car, so you have the magazines, you go to the car shows, and you're talking to your friends about it. You're down at the shop, at the store, looking for the parts you need. You are trying to find just the right color, the cool wheels and rims, and the chrome. You are spending time seeking out whatever it is you want because you're excited about it. It's important to you.

What about hunting season? As the season starts getting closer, hunting guys are seeking. You start gathering your camo and getting your ammo stocked up. You're reading your maps and looking at weather reports. You're online, seeing what's new. You begin stockpiling your supplies while you watch all your hunting shows. You're seeking after it because you want it! You're excited about it.

What do the ladies seek after? You get the dates on your calendar for the big sale that only comes twice a year. You start months in advance looking for the dress for that special event. You start planning, shopping, and preparing all the details for that special party. What about seeking after Mr. Right?! Yes, you're seeking! Don't tell me you don't know how to seek. But, do you seek those things above? We all seek for things we value—are you seeking after God and all the thoughts of God?

Do you plan your schedule around taking time for the things of God? Do you seek time to pray and set aside time for the Word? Do you get excited about worship and going to church? Do you put your time and attention into the things of God? Or do you shrug it off with the thought, *I don't have time for that stuff.*

God wants your heart involved with His Word, in worship, and in prayer. He wants you to keep reading the Scripture. He wants you to get up in the morning and start your day with Him—talking, praying, and confessing the Word—involving Him in your life. I'm talking about really seeking, having a desire to know what He is all about. When you truly want to learn, you do what it takes.

The Bible says in Matthew 3:11, "He [Jesus] will baptize you with the Holy Spirit and fire." He has baptized us with the Holy Spirit and *fire!* If you are born again and filled with the Holy Spirit, you've got the fire of God on the inside of you. Fire is not passive! It makes you get up and move. It makes you *hot*.

It is possible to be filled with passion for the things of God. If you will seek for a spark of excitement about your future, you'll find it. Are you inspired as you look ahead? God created you to live a life filled with inspiration and passion. He created you to live with fire.

In Revelation 3:16, Jesus says, "So then, because you are lukewarm, and neither cold nor hot, I will vomit you out of My mouth". The last thing I want Jesus to call me is lukewarm! He doesn't want you to be lukewarm—He wants you to be hot! He wants you to be passionate, excited, and inspired about His Word and all that He is doing in you. He wants you excited about your life. What kind of fire is in your life? Without passion for the things of God, you will never have the fullness of God operating in your life. You'll have it when you seek for it. It won't fall on you, but it's available to those who seek after things above.

To seek after means to *set your mind* in a new way. That means you may need to move your attention from those areas that have not brought good results to new things. The truth is, if your thoughts are not set on things above, they are always set on the things of this world.

We tend to think that ungodly thoughts are those that are focused on the *really bad* kinds of sin, thoughts of compromising your integrity through lying, cheating, or sexual sin. Your negative thoughts could come from selfishness, greed, or laziness. For most people, the ungodly thoughts that do the most damage are thoughts like, *I just don't care anymore. I give up. It just doesn't matter. It is not going to work.* When you focus on these types of thoughts, you allow doubt, fear, and negativity to control your mind. This is why Paul told us, "Set your mind on things above, not on things on the earth." It is up to you. The choice is yours. By using your God-given free will, you can set your mind on godly thoughts.

Even though I believe it, it is up to *you* to believe you can set your mind where you want it to be—where God wants it to be. Is it easy? No! I'm still working on it. And yet after forty years of practicing, I have seen it work. I can tell you, though, when I first read this scripture as a young Christian, I remember thinking, *That is impossible! You want me to set my mind on things above? Aaah, that's not going to happen!*

I clearly remember when Julius said to me, "Casey, if you could control your mind for one minute, you would be above average."

Today I can make it through about fifty seconds. I'm joking...kind of! The reason it is so hard for the average person to control their thoughts is because of the deeply rooted habits we have developed. From the time we are born, we develop certain routines—thought patterns—that usually include quite a bit of fear, doubt, and other negative thinking. To set your mind on the things of God and never go to the negative is not an easy task.

I recently heard someone talking about a revolutionary new way to exercise. Their theory maintains that the key to successful exercise is intense intervals. They call it *interval training*. The plan is to run full-on, as hard as you can, for two minutes. Then you slow down, jog at a steady pace for one minute and then run as hard as you can for two more minutes. Right now I couldn't run like that at all, let alone for two minutes! Full-on running as hard as I could for two minutes. No way!

You might be in the same boat. There is no way you could run full on for two minutes! You might think, *There is no way I can do that.* The fact is, if you just start somewhere, eventually you *can* do it. Right now, walking a mile might be a strain for you. What if you started with a reasonable goal and stayed with it until you could walk that mile? The day will come when walking a mile will be easy. Maybe walking is easy, but running a mile is impossible. What if you started by taking a few steps? What if you began to run just a little bit? It wouldn't be long until you were running that mile.

As I thought about this principle, it reminded me what it was like when I first began to renew my mind. It is no different than the steps I took as I began to gain control of my thinking. When I first started, I couldn't keep my mind focused for one full minute on the things of God. My thoughts would turn to the world. My mind would be filled with doubt and fear and all the things that I knew weren't right. It took time, but after practicing, dedicating myself, and focusing my thoughts, I began to be able to control my thoughts more and more.

The same is true of your mind. You can become mentally fit—with a mind focused on the things of God. You could say, "I tried that before, and it didn't really work." What if you began to focus your thoughts for a few moments a day, or as the apostle Paul wrote, "*Set your mind* on the things of God"? Do *new thought* interval training. It wouldn't be long until you would be able to set your mind on the things of God more and more throughout your day. Those few small steps would be the beginning of tremendous change in your life.

What would your life look like if you could set your mind on God's thoughts? It would make you a better husband. It would make you a better wife. It would cause you to be able to parent on another level or even do your job and prosper in a new way. You see, many of us want the results but don't want to take the steps to get there. It is similar to losing weight. If you could take a pill and wake up ten pounds lighter, you would do it. However, if you have to discipline your flesh and change your eating habits, it's too hard.

Don't just do what you feel like doing; set your mind on things above. Don't do what you've always done; set your mind on things above. Don't do what your dad did or what your mom did or what's normal in your culture or in your nation; set your mind on things above.

If you could begin to set your mind—and obviously it's possible, or God wouldn't have told you to do it—you'll begin to see a dramatic change in your life. You'll become more and more like Christ. Your faith will be stronger, your mind will be clearer, your gifts will flow, and the blessing of abundant life be manifested in your life. Everything is better when we do things God's way. Do some *mental intervals,* and you'll soon see the change.

Let's clarify what it means to set your mind on the things of God. He is not telling you to walk around all day long thinking about what Heaven looks like. Please! When you are driving your car, don't start thinking about what it is going to look like in Heaven. When you are playing with your children, don't begin thinking about what the throne of God looks like. When you are doing things that need your full attention, make sure you give full attention to those things. I say it like this, "Don't be so heavenly minded, you are no earthly good."

We don't need Christians running around thinking about Heaven and causing accidents. Paul is saying, "Whatever you are doing, have a godly attitude about it." Whatever you're doing, think about it from a godly perspective. How does God want you to work on your job? He wants you to work with all your might. Not just acting right when the boss is around (Ephesians 6:5-6), but doing your very best every moment of every hour. He doesn't want you looking busy only when someone is watching; He wants you to be a productive part of your company all the time. That is setting your mind on things above.

When you are with your wife, how does God want you to think? He wants you to think that you love her as Jesus loves the church. God wants you convinced that you would give all that you have for her. He wants you to give anything and everything to your relationship. What would happen to your marriage if you were to set your mind fully on your spouse?

If you're a man like me, you need to get focused. It's not always easy. Sometimes you just want to watch the game or read that article you've been waiting to read. But if you want to prosper in your marriage and family, you must be willing to set other thoughts and desires aside and *set your mind* on your wife and family.

A Word from Wendy: Coffee Talk

Every day when I came home from school, I would see my mom and dad sitting on the living room couch drinking a cup of coffee and visiting. They called it *coffee time*. I thought all married people did this; so after we were married, I would say to Casey, "Come on, let's sit down and visit." He would look at me like, "What are you talking about?" He didn't have anything like that in his family.

What was normal for me was not for Casey. He had no vision for it, and he honestly had no idea what I was talking about. This brought an immediate sense of conflict and a great opportunity for renewal. Since we both wanted more for our marriage than what we had seen growing up, we had to figure it out. We began to renew our minds to how we wanted our marriage to look, how to have a conversation, and what were we going to talk about.

Conversation is a point of connection. When you're living life with a person you love, you naturally want to know what they are thinking and feeling. You want to know what was funny and who they saw during the time you were apart. You want to connect with them. If you never make room for conversation in your marriage, you're not going to produce the bond that will carry you through the hard times.

The book of James says to be quick to listen and slow to speak. Casey and I, in all the years of our marriage, have had hundreds of conversations because we value our relationship. Did it happen all at once? No. It took time to learn and grow in this area of our marriage. Did Casey always want to stop looking at the TV or put down the magazine? Probably not, but he did it. He put value on the importance of this area of our marriage and renewed his mind to make this a natural and normal part of our daily lives. Placing value on another person by showing them how much you care, brings great strength into the relationship.

Not everyone has been raised in a home with parents who spent time communicating. I have learned over the years that if Wendy asks to visit, I need to set aside whatever else I may be focused on at the moment and *set my mind* on her. Not only has this become vital to me personally, but these times of setting our minds on talking, sharing, and learning more about each other has proven to be richly rewarding and impactful to the strength of our relationship.

How willing are you to do whatever it takes to build your relationship—with God, with your mate, with your children? Can you see how not taking the time to set your mind on God, family, or career causes you to miss insight and opportunities? Setting your mind on things above brings untold rewards into your life.

Ephesians 4:22-24 tells us, "...that you put off, concerning your former conduct, the old man which grows corrupt according to the deceitful lusts, and be renewed in the spirit of your mind, and that you put on the new man which was created according to God, in true righteousness and holiness."

Paul is instructing us to take off the old person, our old ways of living and thinking. We are then told to *put on* the new person, the one created in God's image, according to God's design; the one who is righteous and holy. You might be thinking, *That sounds great, but how do you do that, Paul?* He tells you what you need to do when he says, "Be renewed in the spirit of your mind."

When you are told to *put off* the old person and put on the new person, that speaks of a process—the process of first taking off the old person and then putting on the new person. It's not instantaneous. It is not something that happened the moment you accepted Jesus as Lord. You have to do something more. Putting off the old person is all part of *walking out your own salvation* and is something you have to make happen. It's a process.

The spirit of your mind is stronger than you think. It's controlling your finances. It's controlling your relationships. It's controlling your destiny in every area of your life. We can blame the company and the government, but it's not the people or situations *around* you; it's what is *inside* you that has control over your future.

We could all say we want certain things *around* us to change, but it has to start *in* us. As you are making changes within yourself and you begin to set your mind on things above, you will begin to see the things around you change. The circumstances and your relationships will change—it's amazing! When *you* change, everything in your world changes. It's like you're the center, and whatever is coming out of you is affecting the condition of everyone and everything in your life. When you change, everyone and everything around you changes.

The spirit of your mind is where your thought patterns, habits, and reflex thoughts happen. It's the subconscious, below the surface of your conscious thoughts, where you decide how to live. Just as life at the roots—below the surface—controls how high a plant can grow, or the foundation of a building decides how high it can go, so the spirit of your mind controls how you live, how high you can grow and what you will do.

ELEVEN

You Can Have a Prosperous Soul

> I pray you prosper in all things just as
> your soul prospers.
> —3 John 2

Not long ago we were in an area of the country where the people believe they are the *spiritual vortex* of the world. They also think that if you wear copper or crystals, you will somehow begin to channel a higher level of spiritual power. I rode straight through that vortex on my Harley Davidson, and I have to tell you, I didn't feel any different. I didn't sense any power except that which I was sitting on! To the people who live there and have bought into the story, it is their truth.

Maybe you've met someone who has created their own version of the truth. They have mixed a little bit of Christianity with a little bit of superstition, and thrown in some spiritualism. They may have added a few of the beliefs they picked up from their traditions. If you ask them, they might say their philosophy is based on "a little bit of how I feel, added to a couple of experiences I had. I also read this book about reincarnation—which totally makes sense when you think about it—and well, because this is what I feel." And so it goes. People define *truth* by their own thoughts, in their own way. It's amazing what superstitions and religious traditions people will believe.

"Then Jesus said to those Jews who believed Him, 'If you abide in My word, you are My disciples indeed. And you shall know the truth, and the truth shall make you free'" (John 8:31-32).

The question we need to ask is, "What is the truth?" In many people's lives, the truth is whatever they *think*. The truth is whatever they *feel*. We all know people who say some pretty funny things; and the sad thing is, they honestly think they are speaking the truth.

Jesus told us, "If you abide in My Word, you will know the truth." Did you know that Jesus was called *the truth, the way, and the life*? Not *a* truth but *the* truth. That means there is one way and one truth. What you believe, what you think, your research, and your experience will never overrule the truth of the Word of God. Your truth must have Jesus as the foundation. He is the Word made flesh, and He is the way, the truth, and the life. The Bible reveals Jesus and how we are to live with Him.

In the natural, there are absolute laws that are regarded as truth. Let's take gravity as an example. Every time you jump up into the air, you experience gravity. It is what pulls you back down to the ground. Without gravity, you'd float off into the atmosphere— along with everyone and everything. Gravity is what holds us to the Earth. Everyone knows that is the truth. If you say, "I just don't believe it," guess what? You're still here. Not believing in gravity does not change the truth about gravity. Try jumping off a building, and while you're falling, shout out, "I don't believe in gravity!" As hard as you want to believe it doesn't exist, you are still going to fall!

When something is true, it doesn't matter whether we believe it or not. The same holds true with God. You may say, "I don't believe that God exists." Not to be harsh, but it doesn't matter. Your belief doesn't change the truth. God is still real. Whether you accept Him or not, it does not change the truth. The Bible says that God sent His Son to be your Savior. That's the truth. The Bible says, as a born again believer, the Holy Spirit comes to live in you, dwell in you, and empower your life. The Bible says you can pray the perfect will of God as you pray with the Holy Spirit. You can say, "I don't believe in that," but it doesn't change the fact that it's still true.

As we look at cultures around the world—and the history of those cultures, both past and present—those who follow God's Word and God's truth are those who are prospering. They live with the most freedom and success. We do not often see these people abuse each other. They are not cruel in their laws or the way they govern as a whole. The further a culture gets from God's Word—or from the principles of the Bible—the more abuse, misuse, and disaster that culture will experience.

Third John 3-4 says, "For I rejoiced greatly when brethren came and testified of the truth that is in you, just as you walk in the truth. I have no greater joy than to hear that my children walk in truth."
Jesus put it like this: "If you abide in My Word,...you shall know the truth, and the truth shall make you free." John ties these truths together when he said in III John 2, "Beloved, I pray that you may prosper in all things and be in health, just as your soul prospers." Your soul will prosper as you know the truth, and when you walk in the truth, you become free.

In America, our foundation and prosperity as a nation have always been based on the truth of God's Word. "In God We Trust" has been our motto. Scripture was written into our laws from the very beginning. That's why we need to continue to pray for America. Our biggest problem as a nation right now is that we have moved away from that heritage. We allowed prayer to be taken out of our schools. We reject the Bible and its truths in much of American culture. We find less and less actual truth in our governing laws, and therefore, more and more bondage prevails. Lack of truth puts you in bondage; truth makes you free. As Christians, we are to abide in His Word, and then we will know the truth, and the truth will make us free.

We often place so much stock on what we hear on the news or what the political candidate has to say, but those words should be relatively meaningless in how we live our lives. Personally, I don't listen to them much, and what I do hear I take with a grain of salt. I filter it through the Word of God.

It seems that every few months we hear of another news story that becomes the big news of the day or the week—and eventually we find out it wasn't even true. The spotlight then becomes focused on the reporter who was embellishing their report. We find that they were not telling us the news; they were trying *to be* the news.

Don't let all the drama of current events or politics be the big deal in your life. Keep your mind clear and your heart open to the truth of God's Word. The world is always going to have something to say, but you have to ask yourself, "Do I want to listen?"

What God's Word says is very different than what the world says. What the Word says is meaningful. It has daily and eternal relevance. The Word is something that can change your now—and your forever. So abide in the Word not the words of the world. As you do, you will know *the* truth, and *the* truth will make you free. Connect with the Word, because it affects your soul and you will prosper in all things, even as your soul prospers.

You and I have to decide not only to believe in Jesus and become born again but to embrace what He says. You must embrace His Word and make it more important than anything else—more true to you than what anybody else says. You have to decide that His Word is *the word* upon which your life here on Earth and throughout eternity hangs.

A Word from Wendy: The Easy Pathway

There's something very deceptive about going down the *easy pathway*. Let me tell you the story of a couple who were having some challenges in their marriage. As we were talking, they said, "If we want to work on our marriage, it means we have to renew our minds. We will have to forgive, try to like each other, and talk nicely to each other. That's really hard."

What is your other option? To keep bringing up the past and stay mad. To have long lunches with the guy at work *who really gets you*. Or have a flirtation with an old boyfriend or girlfriend online. The devil puts temptation right in front of you, one that feels good and seems so easy and natural. How can it be wrong, when it feels so right?

God has another pathway. His path is filled with forgiveness, love, and speaking kindly. His path is not as easy. It's not easy to forgive. It is not easy to show kindness towards the person who slammed the door when they walked out on you. It's hard to do the right thing, speak the right words, and rely on God's ways when you don't get the same response from the other person.

As a pastor, I've seen the destruction that comes when a person gives up and decides it's not worth fighting for their marriage. Let me challenge you: Why not fight for the person you committed your life to at one time? You married that person. Sure you have issues you need to work through, but why not fight for your relationship?

More people than I can count have said, "It's not worth it anymore," and my reply is always, "I have seen others take the path that you're headed down, and it's not better. It looks easy now, but in the end you will have all the same problems." They divorce, time goes by, and they meet someone new. She says, "He isn't anything like my first husband." He says, "She is totally different than my last wife." Soon they are on their third or fourth marriage and once again headed to the divorce court. They could have stayed in their first marriage, worked hard, and avoided all the drama and pain.

Doing the right thing is not easy, and the results aren't instantaneous. You will feel like you're doing all the right things and your spouse is not even trying. I have felt that way in my marriage with Casey. I felt like I took all the right actions and he didn't do anything. I felt like I forgave him, but he didn't forgive me. I felt I chose the higher ground, and he didn't. But guess what? He has felt the same way. With over thirty-eight years of marriage, we have had to work through many of the same feelings and negative words that you had with your first marriage; the same words with your second marriage and third marriage. We all have to work through issues—some much harder than others—to renew the spirit of our mind. In the long run, it's worth it to do it God's way.

A prosperous soul causes everything in your life to work the way God planned it to, even family relationships. Why do so many marriages fail? The legal documents state incompatibility as the number one reason—but that is not true. Marriages fail because of a poor soul. When you have a poor soul, your relationship cannot develop in a healthy manner; conflict and problems overwhelm the good, and finally you go your separate ways.

Why is America, and so many Americans, buried in debt? In this rich country, why aren't more of us financially prosperous and stable economically? We have more opportunities for success than most others around the world, but we blame *the economy... and the boss... and the company...* and the list of excuses are endless. It is because so many of us are not prospering in our soul.

You cannot live with wisdom, integrity, and the creativity it takes to succeed in the financial realm without a prosperous soul. When you prosper in your soul, you begin to prosper in all things, including your finances. The prosperity we are talking about does not mean you will become a millionaire. Being rich is not the goal. When you have true prosperity, you will increase in every area, including your finances.

When you have a prosperous soul, you will be able to live the life God has called you to live and be able to help others. That is true prosperity. We have the idea that prosperity is to have millions in the bank, a big house, the fastest car, and unlimited credit. For you, as a Christian, true prosperity is to live as God has called you to live and to help others to do the same. And that begins in your soul.

So many people, even Christians, are stuck in their problems. They wonder, *Why can I not get off the drugs? I can't overcome this addiction! I cannot sustain a long-term relationship.* The same problems keep coming up over and over. It's a soul issue. Your soul is not prospering, and so *you* can't prosper! You need to renew your mind to truth and conquer those things that argue against the Word of God. You must bring every thought into the obedience of Christ. Truth will make you free, and your soul will begin to prosper.

In order to have a prosperous soul, there are five key areas that are critical to your success. If you can renew your thoughts in these areas, you will be able to see and experience a dramatic change in your life.

#1 - Know that God Has a Plan for You.

"Just as He chose us in Him before the foundation of the world, that we should be holy and without blame before Him in love, having predestined us to adoption as sons by Jesus Christ to Himself, according to the good pleasure of His will" (Ephesians 1:4-5).

Many have heard my story of having to deal with Hepatitis C and the eleven months I spent on chemotherapy. I was very discouraged on many levels. I believed in healing, and I preached the Word concerning healing, yet here I was: sick. I'd prayed for so many to be healed. I had spoken the Word over myself and my family for years, and still I was struggling with Hepatitis C.

I felt extremely sick physically during these months of treatments but kept my mind focused on prayer and believing. It was after finally overcoming and getting through it that I got a new perspective. It's been several years since I have been totally cleared of Hepatitis C, and looking back, I can say God used that negative to build more positive into my life. I'm not saying He gave me Hepatitis C. He never wanted me sick. He doesn't give sickness. He doesn't have sickness to give. He has healing. He has health and strength. He gives vitality and long life. All those things come from God because that is who He is.

Sickness wasn't His will for me, but He works every situation—even the negative ones—according to His will. I believe He was saying, "I'm going to use this negative thing that is attacking Casey's life to cause him to have more compassion. We'll use that circumstance to help him to be more understanding, to relate better to those who struggle, to relate even more to those who are sick. We're going to use that negative to build more positive in his life."

Our Father God is so big that He can even use our mistakes and problems to keep moving us towards His plan and His purpose for our lives. What an amazing thought! Can you get your mind wrapped around that? He *chose* you, and He predestined you to be a son or daughter by Jesus Christ, according to the good pleasure of His will.

You are not here by accident. Don't get up in the morning and say, "Well, let's just see what happens." When somebody asks, "How's your life going?" don't let your attitude be, "Well, life happens!" No, *God* happens. God gives purpose. God gives destiny. God gives direction. He's not controlling you, but He is leading and guiding you. He's not dictating everything, but He has a purpose and a plan for you.

Ephesians 1:11 says, "In Him also we have obtained an inheritance, being predestined according to the purpose of Him who works all things according to the counsel of His will."

This scripture doesn't say all things are part of God's will. He said He works "all things" according to His will. It wasn't God's will that I was sick. It wasn't God's will that you were abused. It wasn't His will that you were divorced. God did not want you to have to experience all that you went through when you had your miscarriage. He didn't want you to struggle through that bankruptcy. That wasn't God's plan for your life. But He's so good, and He's so big, that He can use those things to make you better. You gain strength and depth of character as He works *all things according to the counsel of His will*.

You have a destiny. You have a purpose from God. You must believe that. Get your mind wrapped around that thought, because many people never get it. They think their life is an accident. They think their life is just a coincidence. They think the circumstances of their life are just happenstance. You have a calling. You have a destiny. You have a divine purpose from God.

His will is that you be like Christ. He wants you to live on this earth like Jesus did. He wants you to walk in victory—prosper in all things—living a godly life in every possible way. He uses even those negatives to get you to a place that builds compassion, gives understanding for others, and the strength to handle every situation.

When you get up every morning, don't say, "Well, I guess I will try to make a living today." Instead, say with confidence, "I will go out and walk with God today. I will live my destiny and discover the life that God has planned for me. I'm not out doing my thing, but I am doing His thing." It's a powerful way—the biblical way—of looking at your life every day.

#2 - You Control Your Destiny Not the Circumstances Around You.

It's what's in you not what's around you that counts. In spite of knowing that, we tend to blame something else or someone else when things don't go our way. We love to blame, and we come by it honestly. After all, our great-grandfather, thousands of generations back, was the first *blamer*. Way back in the beginning of time, in the Garden of Eden, Adam was the first to start the *blame game*.

As the Lord was out walking in the Garden in the cool of the day, He couldn't find Adam anywhere. God called out, "Hey Adam, where are you?"

Adam said something like, "Whoa, wait a minute, Lord. I just figured out I am naked...and so, well, I'm hiding."

God knew right then, *This is not good!* So He said, "Who told you that you were naked? Did you eat from the tree that I clearly told you not to eat from?"

Adam doesn't even hesitate when he says, "It was the woman that You gave me. She made me eat it!" (See Genesis 3:1-19.)

Adam did not miss a beat as he blamed his wife, blamed the devil, and blamed the Lord. And we've been doing the same thing ever since, haven't we? We blame our wives, blame our husbands, blame the boss, and if nothing else is working for us, we blame God. We think things like, *God made me this way. It's just the way I am. I can't help it. I was born this way.*

We like to pretend it's God's fault that we're stupid, broke, or miserable. We love to blame. Who's your favorite person to blame? Your spouse? Your children? When your friend asks, "Why were you late to church today?" do you quickly reply, "Well, you know how it is with the kids"?

Who or what do you blame most often when you need an excuse? Your marriage? Your job? Your health? I think we often create whatever story works best for us, and then we convince ourselves that it's true. That's the bad part. When you are building your life by blaming others, you actually have to believe it. Why don't you work out more? "Well, the boss, and the job, and the wife, and the kids." So, it's all their fault that you're unhealthy? Why don't you eat healthier food? "Well, you know…I can't afford it…and McDonalds...and the grocery store…and my kids…."

We all do it. We all have something or someone we can blame our condition on. What if you could just accept that every action you take is a choice—and the choice is up to you? Don't think of this as a burden, but as an opportunity to change. Don't consider this a way to make yourself feel bad, but as a way to empower your new life.

One day as I sat in the Rehab Center with Julius, we began talking about my current circumstances. I was on probation, had several state fines to pay off, and a judge had just ordered me to do community service. It was all weighing on me, and I was feeling bad. Julius said to me, "You'll overcome all those things just as soon as you take responsibility." It was one of the most empowering moments of my life.

What Julius said to me that day—and the way he said it—became one of the greatest revelations of my life. With that revelation came an amazing sense of, *I can do this*. When you have a lifetime of feeling down and out, it's an incredible feeling to realize that deep down inside, *I can overcome. I can succeed in life. I can do this.*

At that moment, I knew I had to take responsibility and acknowledge my own decisions had caused the problems in my life. I knew that I could no longer blame others—for anything. The moment I accepted responsibility, I felt incredibly free. With that freedom came the sense of knowing that, for the first time, I could do something different with my life.

If you cannot assume responsibility for your actions, you will never have authority over your life. You are rendered helpless. You cannot do anything to change the life that you're living without taking responsibility for yourself. If you believe others control your life, you stay down, you stay sad, and you stay weak. When you take full responsibility, suddenly you can take authority over your situation.

You have the ability to handle every problem.

A Word from Wendy: Why Live Holy?

Why is it important to live differently than the world? Why do you want to think and act differently? In reality, smoking, drinking, and overeating are not evil. There are many good people who have unhealthy habits. They are not good for your body, and may cause harm to others, but they won't keep you out of Heaven. It isn't about the smoking or the drinking. It's about the example.

The first time I recognized the power of the message I was sending was when my friend confronted me for trying to get her saved while smoking my cigarette. When my friend looked at me, she judged me as a hypocrite; and because of my example, I could not lead her to Jesus. I said I was a Christian, yet I was still smoking, which in her eyes made me a bad example.

There are many reasons why smoking is bad for you, but as I said, it won't send you to Hell. I only quit smoking because I loved a person more than I loved the act. I believe that because the desire of my heart was to help someone else know Him, the grace of God gave me the strength to quit.

As Christians, we renew our minds to become a higher influence in peoples' lives. Being mean-spirited won't send you to Hell. It just doesn't make you a shining light for Jesus. If you are a person who is always angry, it won't stop you from going to Heaven. Your anger will simply stop people from listening to you or wanting to follow you. You can't show the love of God and express anger at the same time. You can't say you are a Christian, act like the world, and then expect others to be drawn to Christ. Renewing your mind is about loving people more than loving the thing inside of you that is not godly. You want to change it so that you can be a stronger witness for Jesus.

As soon as you decide, *It's my life, and I'm going to take responsibility for it*, you will find new strength. Your spirit and your soul will start rising up, and a new perspective will begin to form in your heart. That one decision will create a new vision, a new way of seeing yourself and your life. You will start to win.

You will win in life because of what has happened in your heart not because something *out there* is different. You'll succeed because of what's in you not because of what's around you. You'll prosper because your spirit and your soul are healthy. It will no longer be about what anyone else does or doesn't do. It's now about what you and God are doing. You and God will decide your destiny not the circumstances around you.

Second Corinthians 4:16-18 tells us, "Therefore we do not lose heart. Even though our outward man is perishing, yet the inward man is being renewed day by day. For our light affliction, which is but for a moment, is working for us a far more exceeding and eternal weight of glory, while we do not look at things which are seen, but at the things which are not seen. For the things which are seen are temporary, but the things which are not seen are eternal."

In other words, although these pressures are momentary, they're working for you a *far more exceeding and eternal weight of glory*. When you look from the perspective of God's Word, you are not going to look at your situation through eyes of blame. You are going to look to the Lord to lead and guide you through. You will look to the promise not at the problem.

Do not look at those things *which are seen* and blame them for the way you are. Look to the things which are *not seen*. Look at the spiritual things, the eternal things, the internal things. Your faith, heart, passion, and compassion—these are what will decide your destiny!

When we blame the current president for the way things are, what are we going to do when we elect the next president? We blame the boss, but what about when we get the next boss? We blame our neighbor, but what happens when we get the new neighbor? Once we start the blame game, we've lost the power to change and given up control of our destiny.

Take responsibility and believe in your heart: *God and I are walking this out. God and I are on this journey. God and I can beat this addiction. God and I can overcome this bankruptcy. God and I can get through this divorce.* Whatever the challenge—now you've got the power of Heaven on your side! Power comes from taking responsibility. Do not allow what is around you to limit you; let what is in you to lead your life. Then you will be transformed by the renewing of your mind and on your way to a prosperous soul—and His perfect will.

#3 - It's God's Will that You Prosper in All Things and Live an Abundant Life.

How did Jesus live when He walked on Earth? Modern religion tells us He was poor and barely had enough to get by. Traditionally, we think of Him as a man who lived outdoors, in the fields of Israel, with nothing. We've all seen the pictures of Him dressed in the white gown, holding a staff in one hand and a baby lamb in His arms. He wore simple clothing and lived a simple life. The problem is, my Bible tells me a different story than tradition would lead us to believe.

Jesus had more than enough. He was always blessing those around Him. He was filling up boats with fish and filling baskets with leftover bread. Jesus always provided more than enough and lived in abundance. He had a treasurer and a treasury. Although this is not the traditional view of His life, that is how Jesus lived; and we're supposed to be like Him. First John 4:17 tells us, "As He is, so are we in this world." The Scriptures are very direct in this issue. From the Old Testament to the New Testament, we see over and over that it is God's will for us to prosper.

God said in Joshua 1:8, "This Book of the Law shall not depart from your mouth, but you shall meditate in it day and night, that you may observe to do according to all that is written in it. For then you will make your way prosperous, and then you will have good success." It is God's will that you prosper and have success. He would not tell you how to prosper if it was not His will. And the key to your success is His Word.

It's amazing how hard we often make things, and yet God is so very clear. He tells us exactly *what* He wants us to do, and then He tells us *how* it will affect our lives. "Walk in My Word. Meditate on My Word. Observe to do My Word. You will prosper. You will have good success."

In John 10:10, Jesus said, "I have come that they may have life, and that they may have it more abundantly." The word *abundantly* literally means plentiful, amply supplied, existing or occurring in large amounts. The best and the most. That's God's will for His children. He wants us to have the best of what is available and more than enough to meet not only our own needs but to be a blessing to others. That is true abundance.

Here is the real question: What defines *abundant life* to you? Many would quickly say, "I want an abundance of money. If I won the Lottery, then I would have more than enough. I wouldn't have to worry about money ever again!" Sure, having enough money to pay your bills and having extra would be considered abundance. But, is that true abundance? What about the abundance of having your material needs met *and* having your health? How about having a healthy, happy family that loves God, loves each other, and shows God's love by helping others? Is that considered abundance? What about being part of a church that impacts your community and your city?

What tops the list of what you consider living in abundance? Not comparing yourself to others or adopting what they believe is important would be a good place to start. Rather than look at what others desire, ask yourself, *What do I desire in my heart*? When you compare yourself to everybody around you, you are not living in the true abundance that comes from the heart of Father God. When you find out what God has for you and listen to your own heart, you will receive His true abundance.

In III John 2, John said, "Beloved, I pray that you may prosper in all things and be in health, just as your soul prospers." Do you think John would pray that prayer if it was not God's will for us to prosper in all things? John was an apostle. In fact, he was the oldest living apostle when he wrote this passage of Scripture. He was the great apostle John, who lived on the island of Patmos as he wrote the book of Revelation, along with several other major books of the New Testament. Don't you agree that, of all people, John would know God's will?

Many have been taught that God wants you to struggle and be poor. Were you led to believe God wants you to suffer from sickness and pain? That is wrong thinking. How do I know it is wrong thinking?

It does not line up with what the Bible teaches. If your thinking is not in line with what God's Word teaches, you will never have His abundance—or His will. Joy, peace, prosperity, and an abundant life are what God wants for you. His desire is for you to prosper *in all things*, to live in health and have an abundant life.

I believe these *Seven Keys to a Prosperous Soul* will strengthen and help you as you take the next steps in your life. Take time to implement these truths into your daily walk with Christ.

1. A prosperous soul hungers for and desires the Word of God (Matthew 5:6).
2. A prosperous soul meditates or ponders the Word of God daily (Psalm 1:1-3).
3. A prosperous soul is following the *inner* man/woman (or spirit) not the flesh or emotions (Romans 8:6).
4. A prosperous soul maintains a godly and positive attitude, even in challenging circumstances (Matthew 6:33).
5. A prosperous soul seeks to grow and improve, even to the point of confessing faults (James 5:16).
6. A prosperous soul knows that life on Earth is temporary, and we are to set our minds on the things of Heaven (Colossians 3:1-2).
7. A prosperous soul knows that God's Word is the truth and is higher than every other "truth," even emotions, culture, and traditions (John 8:31-32).

There's only one way we can really know the will of God, and that is by knowing the Word of God. You can't find God's will by looking at the world. You can't find God's will by looking at what you feel, because feelings change. One day you're up and one day you're down; your emotions will come and go. But God's Word will remain the same. You can only know God's will through God's Word.

You can only have the abundant life God promised you as you identify and change your wrong thinking. You must be transformed by the renewing of your mind so you can live in His perfect will. Get your mind set on the truth of what God has for you: *God wants me to win. God wants me to prosper. God wants me to live an abundant life.* God wants you to prosper in all things and live an abundant life.

That's God's plan.

#4 - God Desires Order and Balance in Your Life.

"Let all things be done decently and in order" (I Corinthians 14:40).

I Corinthians 14:40

God is a God of order and balance, and He desires order and balance in your life as well. He has said, let *all* things—every part of your family life, financial life, and ministry/church life—be done decently and in order. There's an order to the ways things should be done. There is a right way to do things, and there is a wrong way. God is very specific about how we are to live our lives.

Order means right priorities and keeping our schedule balanced. Faith, family, work, fun—they all have a place in life. Church attendance, volunteering, and serving are all part of the order in a godly life. It is a vital part of our Christian life and should not be neglected. Although going to church and serving is a good thing, it has to be done *decently and in order*. You have to decide what your priorities are and establish a proper balance in your life. I feel that many of us are always slightly or even *way* out of balance.

As a whole, most of us in America live our lives out of balance. We easily accept as normal the hours spent commuting and working, but how many hours are allotted to be with the children? How many hours are spent with our spouse? Hours traveling for our job is necessary, but how many hours do we also spend in prayer, worship, and Bible study? We may say, "I haven't got time for that! I have to get to work so that I can pay my bills. That has to come first, and by the time I get home, I am too exhausted to do anything more!" That, my friend, is a life tragically out of balance.

You don't want to give so much to one area of your life that everything else suffers. As a parent, you don't want to give so much to your child that everything else falls by the wayside. You cannot raise a successful child if they believe they are the center of the universe— because they're not. If you allow them to control the schedule, the house, the food, and you, you are in big trouble. You need order and balance, even with your children.

Your children need to know that loving God and spending time with Him is your *first* priority. Your spouse is next on the list of priorities. Then your children, your job, and church life fill out the list of your top priorities. You will also want to add things like recreation, friendships, physical fitness, and hobbies to the list of your priorities. We are talking about living a well-balanced life.

A child-centered home is not a healthy home. Your children need to realize that they've got to fit into the big picture, because everything does not revolve around them. There will come a day when your child will come to a rude awakening and learn that they are not the center of the universe. There will always be someone out there who will share that information with them, and more than likely, it will not be in the same spirit of love that you would use.

It is so much easier on your children if you are the one to teach them that's it's important to learn to respect others, give and not just get, and not get their way all the time. When you create a child-centered way of life, you are setting your child up for failure. Keep balance and order as the focus of your godly priorities. It will keep you and them on the path to a success-filled life.

The other day I was with one of our doctors, who shared an interesting thought with me. We have all heard that, as we get older, our bones become fragile. When we fall, there is much more damage done than when we were younger. What my friend was saying was, as we mature and have issues with broken bones, the problem isn't so much fragility of the bones but a lack of balance.

We will stumble or trip, and suddenly we will fall. As a result, we end up with a broken hip or a broken wrist. The next time, it's a broken shoulder. Yes, the bones have become more fragile and break more easily, but the main problem is a lack of balance.

A *lack of balance* causes problems in your physical body and in every area of your life. How's your balance? The way you balance your life may decide whether something *gets broken* or not. It may determine whether your children are strong and healthy or not. Your balance may be the deciding factor in your destiny, because God said that all things should be done decently and in order.

#5 - Excellence Empowers You to Overcome Every Negative.
"O Lord, our Lord, How excellent is Your name in all the earth" (Psalm 8:1).

God loves excellence. The Lord is *the most* excellent; excellence is His nature. Excelling is part of His character. What He does is *always* excellent. Can you imagine what it would be like if God had a bad day? You would hope that it wasn't the day He created you, right? The truth is, He doesn't have a bad day. He doesn't have a shoddy day, then a lukewarm day, a half-hearted day, then a better day, and ending the week with an excellent day. Can you imagine what we would be like if that were the case? No, every day God has is excellent. If we are walking with Him, we can be excellent too.

Obviously, you are human, and you live in this world, so you are never going to be perfect. You will never have it all together and do everything perfectly, the way God does it. That doesn't mean you can't try to do your best. It doesn't mean you can't strive to have the same excellent spirit as your Father God.

Having an excellent spirit is just one more part of your journey toward renewing your mind. Don't just *try to get by*. You are not just attempting to survive. You don't have a lukewarm, half-hearted mentality about the things that you do. Whatever you do, you do it wholeheartedly, as unto the Lord (Colossians 3:23). Reach for God's best with all that is within you. Seek to excel.

When you are parenting, be the best parent possible. When you are taking care of your home, strive to create an excellent environment: clean, well-ordered, and peaceful. When you are at the job, be an excellent employee, one who is looked up to as a good role-model.

So many people, even Christians, are half-hearted in their efforts.

They are never all-in. They have the attitude of: *Well, we'll see. Let's give it a try. I'll check it out.* So their lives become lukewarm. Jesus told us that He would rather have us hot or cold but not lukewarm (Revelation 3:15-16).

Are you lukewarm in the way you live your life? How do you take care of your home? Your car? Your clothing? How do you watch over the various areas of your life—of your world? Are you lukewarm about the way you conduct yourself at work? Are you lukewarm toward your marriage and your children? Do you take care of yourself physically in a half-hearted manner? Excellence is about being engaged in every aspect of your life. A spirit of excellence empowers you to overcome every negative thing.

When I think of an example of excellence, I always look to the book of Daniel. First, we have to remember that Daniel was a refugee. His parents were killed when Babylon invaded Jerusalem.

Nebuchadnezzar, the King of Babylon, instructed the Babylonians to kill all the Jewish elders and to bring the brightest and the best of the young people back to Babylon. The evil king wanted only "young men in whom there was no blemish, but good-looking, gifted in all wisdom, possessing knowledge and quick to understand" (Daniel 1:4). He wanted only the best of the young men for his kingdom.

Daniel was a part of Nebuchadnezzar's group of excellent young men. As the story unfolds, Daniel is an orphan and a refugee. Not only has he physically lost everything he is familiar with, but he is also now living in a country that does not recognize or honor his God. Daniel is trying to stand up for what he believes in a world where he has lost everything. Nothing in his world is the same. It is all so different and so contrary to what he is used to. In the midst of all this tragedy and change, Daniel stood out from all the rest.

Daniel didn't fit in, and he definitely didn't follow the crowd. In Daniel 1:5, the king decreed that only certain food and wine be given to these young men as they were prepared to serve him. He also set up three years of rigorous training as part of the very specific plan he had put into place. But Daniel did not just fall in with what his new world dictated. In verse 8, Daniel purposed not to defile his heart and requested different food and drink from the rest.

If you read through the rest of Daniel, chapter one, you will find that he stood up for what he knew was right and did not go along with what was easy. He proved himself to those in charge, and by the end of the training period, there were none among them all like Daniel and his three friends, Hananiah, Mishael, and Azariah (whom we know as Shadrach, Meshach, and Abednego). Daniel 1:20 says, "And in all matters of wisdom and understanding about which the king examined them, he found them ten times better than all the magicians and astrologers who were in all his realm."

After many years, a lot of drama, and a new king, the story continues. The new king was having a problem. He had a strange dream and was seeking the interpretation. When all else failed, he called for Daniel. Daniel 5:12 says, "Inasmuch as an excellent spirit, knowledge, understanding, interpreting dreams, solving riddles, and explaining enigmas were found in this Daniel, whom the king named Belteshazzar, now let

Daniel be called, and he will give the interpretation."

Because of his excellent spirit, Daniel was able to overcome all the negatives around him. He had an excellent prayer life and habits.

He was the leader of his friends and the one everyone looked to when they needed answers. Daniel never bowed down to the world, never gave up when faced with overwhelming odds, and he will forever be known as the one with an *excellent spirit.*

Think *excellence* in everything you do, *excellence* in how you carry yourself and go about your business. When you raise the bar to one of *excellence,* God will raise you up. If you keep thinking only of survival, with the mentality of, *I'll do just enough to get by,* you will never go beyond average. Don't let your mind conform to the world's ways. Don't be the one who thinks, *I'm not going to do more, because no one else is doing more around here. I'm not going to do any better, because no one else does any better around here. I'm just going to do what everybody else does, because I get tired just thinking about doing more.* If you have that *get by* mentality, you are stuck.

Just like Daniel, you can determine, *I'm going to have an excellent spirit. I'm going to excel and go above what is considered average. To the best of my ability, I'm going to be excellent in everything I do.* Watch how God will prosper you when you decide to be different, the one with an *excellent spirit.*

TWELVE

Pressing Toward Your Future

> I give you a future and a hope.
> —Jeremiah 29:11

There was once a young boy walking down the road when he came upon a frog. The boy picked up the frog, and as he continued to walk, the frog began to talk to him. He said, "Hey boy! This is your blessed day. I am a miracle frog. If you kiss me, I'll turn into a princess. I'll love you forever, and we'll live happily ever after." The little boy's eyes lit up, and he smiled so big. Then he stuffed that frog down into his pocket, and he just kept on walking. Soon the frog crawled out of the pocket and stuck out his long tongue and licked the side of the boy's face and he said, "Hey boy! I'm a miracle frog!. Kiss me, and I'll turn into a princess. I'll love you forever, and we'll live happily ever after." The little boy just smiled again and kept on walking. Well, this time, the frog stuck out his long tongue and just slapped the side of the boy's face and said, "Hey! What's wrong with you? Kiss me! I'll turn into a princess. I'll love you forever, and we'll live happily ever after." Well, the boy took hold of the frog and brought him right up to his eyes, and he said, "Frog, I heard you the first time, but I'm only eight years old. I don't want a princess. I want a talking frog!"

Here is my question for you, *Is God trying to give you a prince or a princess, but you're focused on a talking frog?* Maybe God has more for your life than you've ever thought. Maybe His plan and destiny for you are much bigger, much richer, and much more fulfilling than you've ever imagined.

How many times did Jesus say to people, "What can I do for you? What do you want from me? What is it that you're seeking?" Why did the Lord ask those questions when the answers always seemed so obvious?

In Mark 10:46-52, a blind man named Bartimaeus heard that Jesus was near. He began to shout, "Jesus, Son of David, have mercy on me!" People around Bart told him to be quiet, but he just shouted louder. Jesus heard him shouting, and He stood still—and then He asked that Bart be brought to Him. Jesus did something that might seem perplexing to most of us. He said, "What do you want me to do for you?"

Didn't the Lord know what *blind* Bartimaeus wanted? It was obvious he wanted his sight restored, wasn't it? It might have been, but I believe the Lord is making an important point. He is teaching us the value in clearly and openly expressing our desires. What do you need? What you are living for, and what do you want in life? Blind Bartimaeus might have asked for anything from the Lord, but he wanted his sight. Jesus required him to ask, to clearly say what he wanted.

Our thoughts often get trapped in the wrong places as we walk through life. Maybe your thoughts have become unfocused. Your vision is no longer clear. You are thinking about the wrong things. You've lost sight of all God has for you.

A Word from Wendy: Who Do You Think You Are?

Even as a child, I had a strong desire to lead. I clearly remember having to move when I was seven years old. Our family always moved at the beginning of summer, when there was no school in session. This was the worst time to move because, in our new home, I wouldn't have any friends to play with for the summer. Since we all wanted friends to play with, my oldest sister said to me, "Come on, let's go door-to-door and see if we can find any friends. But Wendy, you're the one who has to do the talking, because you're the one who does that kind of thing."

Now mind you, I'm not the oldest. I was only in the second grade with my two older siblings. As we walked up to the door, visualize this: Four little, darling kids at your door, saying, "Are there any children in your house that we could play with?" I would feel bad if I had to say no to all that cuteness!

The natural bent of my personality was to be a leader, but by the time I got into high school, that little girl was gone. The girl who was willing to knock on the door and be a leader wasn't that person anymore. I had started viewing myself through a very small lens. I began to think, "You can't do that." So I did nothing. I just basically kept myself in my own little world, didn't have any high expectations, and didn't go very far.

I look at my life and think, isn't that amazing, how the devil so subtly stole my self-worth, my energy, and my outgoing personality. I wasn't doing anything terrible; I just didn't do anything good either! How many of us were not wild and crazy? We were not out there like my husband was, getting arrested, busting up cars, and waking up in jail. But we were not doing anything positive either.

The devil comes to steal, kill and destroy. Jesus came to give us life—abundant life (John 10:10)! Renewing your mind to God's ways will bring back into focus those areas of gifting that have gotten blurry over time. He has a wonderful plan for you; it is up to you to grab hold of it!

You say, "Pastor Casey, don't you love me the way I am?" Yes, I do, and God loves you the way you are too! He also loves you enough not to leave you the way you are. Sure, I love you the way you are. You love me the way I am, but you don't want me to stay this way forever. You hope I continue to learn the Word and become a better Christian. You probably hope I mature, and I'm sure you hope I keep becoming more like Jesus.

I loved my children when they were five years old, but I didn't want them to stay five years old forever. As cute as that age was, acting like a five-year-old would not be cute at age fifteen. I loved my children when they reached every age, but I'm glad they're not still acting like that now. We all have to continue growing and moving forward in life.

As human beings, we are designed to move forward. When you feel like you're not getting better—your life is going nowhere—that is when you start getting discouraged. You begin to feel hopeless. That feeling of stagnation violates your very nature. It goes against everything God put within you. Remember, you are made in the likeness and image of God. When you're moving forward—filled with hope, dreams, and vision—life is good.

Most of us love the beginning of a new year. We're making big plans, setting goals, and filled with fresh inspiration for what lies ahead. We see ourselves taking new risks. Many have just started college or are off to the new job, and life is exciting.

It seems that the younger you are, the more excited you are for the new year and all that it will bring. But as we mature, we often disconnect from the excitement of vision and dreams. We stop renewing our minds. We stop learning and growing, so life becomes stagnant and we begin to feel hopeless.

That feeling of hopelessness you often have when you have no vision brings with it a feeling of helplessness. When you feel helpless, you start looking for ways to get away from your pain. You start finding ways to check out—to find a new spouse, a new job, a new girlfriend, or a new credit card.

When you feel helpless, you naturally begin to explore ways to medicate your pain, whether it is through drugs, alcohol, sex, or even food. You say to yourself, "Maybe I'll just watch more TV.

Maybe I'll drink more. Maybe I'll take some medication. Maybe I'll take some drugs. Maybe I'll just do something crazy like go online and find out what my old high school boyfriend is doing!" Have you lost your mind? Yes, you have! If you're not daily creating the vision for your life with God's Word, you're losing the battle for your mind!

God said to Abraham in Genesis 13:14, "Lift your eyes now and look." What if you could look up and *see* all that God has for you? It's possible. I am not talking about cars or houses. Those things are just natural, material things that help us see what is possible in other realms as well. God has so much more for us than just natural things. And what is possible in the natural realm is possible in other areas of your life. You can raise your vision and have something different in *every* part of your life—spirit, soul, and body. Lift up your eyes and you will see your promised land.

Do you remember what happened as the nation of Israel stood on the border of the Promised Land? The story is found in Numbers, chapter 13. The Lord spoke to Moses in verses 1 and 2 and told him to send some men to spy out the land of Canaan. Obeying God's command, Moses sent twelve spies. One spy was chosen from each of the twelve tribes. When the twelve spies came back, ten of them gave a bad report. Numbers 13:27-28 says, "Then they told him, and said: "We went to the land where you sent us. It truly flows with milk and honey, and this is its fruit. Nevertheless the people who dwell in the land are strong; the cities are fortified and very large; moreover we saw the descendants of Anak there.*"*

The spies were excited about all the land had to offer. It was awesome. They were struck with the abundance of provision and great beauty. The Bible says, "It truly flows with milk and honey." They brought back some of the fruit to show how much better it was than anything they had ever seen. The land God had promised them was beyond all they could have imagined.

But, as they were raving about the land, ten of the spies gave a negative report. Not only were they filled with awe at the richness of the land, but also they were filled with fear, trepidation, and doubt. Instead of remembering that God had promised them this land, they allowed their senses to take over. Looking with their eyes instead of their hearts, they only saw that there were giants among the people and that the cities were well fortified. Instead of looking through eyes of faith, they looked through their natural eyes—and could not *see* any way to possess the land. In verse 33, they said, "There we saw the giants (the descendants of Anak came from the giants); and we were like grasshoppers in our own sight, and so we were in their sight." Their minds were made up. Their minds were filled with all the reasons they could not take the land. Because of doubt, they were robbed of all God had promised them.

Even as the ten spies convinced themselves and the people that they would never claim their Promised Land, there were two spies with a different story. Caleb and Joshua came back with a different report.

Numbers 13:30 says, "Then Caleb quieted the people before Moses, and said, 'Let us go up at once and take possession, for we are well able to overcome it.'"

Caleb and Joshua said, "We can do this." They were ready to possess the land, but the rest of the spies spoke negatively and convinced the people that it was impossible. The people of Israel had been slaves for so long that, even though they had been taken out of slavery, the slavery mentality was still in them. They looked at all the land had to offer and saw something they could not imagine possessing. They did not look through eyes of faith at the promise of God; they only saw their own inability. They said among themselves, "It's too good to be true. It's too big. It's too amazing." They believed they could never live in a place like that. They looked at the outward situation and did not *see* any way to overcome it.

In Numbers 14:24 the Bible tells us, "But My servant Caleb, because he has a different spirit in him and has followed Me fully, I will bring into the land where he went, and his descendants shall inherit it." Caleb had said, "Let us go up. We can win the battle. We can overcome." But it was too much for the people. They could not believe. They could not possess the Promised Land by faith, and they *did not* possess it in the natural. Caleb and Joshua were the only ones to enter in.

God told the nation of Israel in Numbers 14:30, "Except for Caleb the son of Jephunneh and Joshua the son of Nun, you shall by no means enter the land which I swore I would make you dwell in." The whole nation missed out on entering into the Promised Land because they could not renew their minds to God's promises. At eighty-five years old, Caleb possessed his mountain in the Promised Land.

No doubt you have seen it happen today: those who have gotten out of poverty, but the poverty is still in them. Many have gotten out of an abusive situation, but the abuse is still in them. A person who has overcome being victimized, but they still have a victim's mentality. So it was with Israel. They were free from Egypt, but slavery was still in them.

Remember what they said? "There are giants in the land, and we are like grasshoppers." Not only did the children of Israel think the inhabitants of the land saw them as grasshoppers, but also that's the way they saw themselves. They saw themselves as grasshoppers. These are the same people who had just been delivered from slavery by God. They had gone through the Red Sea! God gave them a pillar of fire by night and a pillar of cloud by day. They had miracles, they had manna, and they had water flowing out of a rock. Still, they could not believe.

The nation of Israel had seen first-hand the deliverance of God. He had performed supernatural miracles on their behalf, yet the spirit of their mind was still dark and small. The spirit of their mind was filled with, *We're poor people, and there is no way we can have our own land. Besides that, we're like grasshoppers*. That's what they said because that thinking was in them. Their belief—and yours—comes out of the heart, first in thoughts, then manifested in words and through actions.

Caleb and Joshua were different than the rest! They said, "Come on! We can overcome because God is with us." They weren't promoting their own idea; they were standing on God's promise for this situation. The Israelites would not believe. Therefore, not one adult over the age of twenty was able to enter the Promised Land except Joshua and Caleb. Forty years later, just as the Lord had commanded, the people went in and possessed the Promised Land.

What a tragedy! Look at the number of people who missed out on their Promised Land. How many today miss their destiny? It is not an identical situation, but how many miss what God has for them simply because the spirit of their mind cannot accept it? They just can't believe. They say, "I have a hard time wrapping my mind around that." Well, okay...then you can't have it. If you can't get your mind around it, you can't have it. If you want to inherit the promises of God, you need to get your mind around something bigger. You've got to see it as God's will.

We often accept as normal things that are directly opposed to God's Word. We cannot enter into our promised land—which includes every promise written in the Word of God—when we do not embrace all of God's promises. How many of those promises have you actually possessed? Or, like the Israelites, how many do you see as *too big* for you to have?

God promises us a healthy body, and that we would live a long and healthy life. That's His promise to us, but how many people talk themselves into being sick. When talking about physical ailments they say things like, "My sickness, my headache, my back pain, my cancer, my diabetes." They can't wait to tell you, "My diabetes is just getting worse every year." We name it, claim it, and then we hang onto it.

Having a *mentality of sickness* is common. Sickness has become a way of life, especially in those countries that are most civilized. By civilized, I mean those countries with the best technology, media, and medicine. In America we are constantly hearing about sickness and the medicine we need to cure us. Of course, if the sickness or medicine does not kill us, the side effects will. We hear about sickness 24/7, and then we wonder why we never get healed. What if you fed the spirit of your mind only thoughts of healing and wellness. Consider what might happen if you daily confessed, "I am healed in the name of Jesus. By His Stripes I have been made whole."

First Peter 2:24 says, "Who Himself bore our sins in His own body on the tree, that we, having died to sins, might live for righteousness— by whose stripes you were healed." What if you renewed the *spirit of your mind* about your health, about your strength and vitality? What would happen? You would walk a little faster. You would look for stairs to climb instead of an escalator. You would begin to enjoy working out, and you would live a longer, healthier life. You would begin to *feel* healthy, and you would *be* healthy. Remember, *as a man thinks in his heart, so is he* (Proverbs 23:7). The battle that you and I are fighting is to walk daily into God's promised land.

Numbers 14:18 says, "The LORD is longsuffering and abundant in mercy, forgiving iniquity and transgression; but He by no means clears the guilty, visiting the iniquity of the fathers on the children to the third and fourth generation."

This statement seems like a contradiction, doesn't it? This scripture is telling us that God is longsuffering and abundant in mercy, but He holds the sins of the fathers against the children to the second, third, and fourth generation. That doesn't seem merciful or even fair! When I see a scripture that does not make sense, I take another look to see what I can learn. Let's look a little deeper.

God isn't talking about holding you personally responsible for a mistake your dad made in the past. That would not be fair, and it is not something He would do. What this scripture is talking about is that the negativity you were raised with—that you lived with and accepted—will stay with you.

If you were raised in a home of divorce, statistics show you're likely to become divorced. If you're raised in an alcoholic home, statistics tell us you're likely to become an alcoholic. It's not 100 percent fact, but your chances are much higher because of the way you were raised. It takes a conscious decision to renew the spirit of your mind, or you will end up in the same circumstances as your parents, and their parents, and their parents before them. The Bible says in Proverbs 22:6, "Train up a child in the way he should go, and when he is old he will not depart from it." We could also say, "Train up a child in the way he should *not* go, and when he is old, he won't depart from that either."

A Word from Wendy: Rejoice in Yourself Alone

Arriving at Bible college was both exciting and nerve-wracking, and I was so ready to get started in this new life. I was looking forward to meeting my new roommate. Finally, I would have someone who was heading the same direction, wanting to learn the things of God. After getting settled in, one of our first decisions as roommates was that we would sit on our beds each night and read the Bible together.

One night, I found a scripture that became the cornerstone of my walk with Christ. It was Galatians 6:4, and it says: "But let each one examine his own work, and then he will have rejoicing in himself alone, and not in another." This one verse would revolutionize my life. I still remember the impact I felt the first time I read it over forty years ago. When I read—*rejoice in yourself alone*—it opened up something in my life that God continuously speaks into my heart. Over and over, that still small voice has said, "Quit judging yourself. Learn how to love the gifting, the calling, the strength within you."

When I looked at my older sister, who is now a school teacher, I always thought, *I will never be as good as her*. I thought many times, *My brother is a very smart businessman and so much smarter than I am*. Just as I was drowning in comparison with my older siblings, the Word of God taught me to *rejoice in myself alone and not in another*. He said to me, "Wendy, stop trying to line yourself up in personality, style, and gifting with these people." I could see that I was not like my sister, but I thought she was *better* than me, so I tried to be like her. I tried to be like my brother because I thought he was *better* than me.

How many of us walk down this type of pathway all of our life? Someone else is always *better*. You always look at them and think, "Why can't I be like them? Why can't I look like them?" God says, "No, no, no, Honey. I need you to start thinking the way I think about you."

Jeremiah 1:5 says, "Before I formed you in the womb I knew you; Before you were born I sanctified you." Psalm 139:13 says, "For You have formed my inward parts; You covered me in my mother's womb."

God's Word and His Spirit have helped me to renew my mind and have given me the ability to think differently about myself. The Bible says in Matthew 22:37-39 that we are to *love God and love our neighbors as we love ourselves*. You can't love your neighbor if you don't love yourself. It's impossible to love someone you are always comparing yourself with. Allow God to show you how He sees you. You are uniquely made, one-of-a-kind, and created with His purpose in mind.

What have you picked up from your childhood that is hindering you? Don't let the sins of your *fathers* be passed on to the next generation. You have the ability to stop them. I love it when I see people make changes in their lives and overcome the past they were once bound to. One of my close friends came from a background of alcoholism, divorce, abuse, and negativity. He broke the sins that would have been passed through him to his family. He has taken seriously his responsibility to break that negative heritage and is now passing on a new destiny to his own children. Why? Because he saw the value in God's Word and the difference it could make in his life. What he has done, with the help of the Holy Spirit, means his children will now go out with a new spirit in their minds and the presence of God in their lives. What an awesome thing: to break that negative spirit and pass on something better to the next generation.

As parents, we want to give the next generation a chance to walk into their promised land. We want them to have a chance at a better life. We want to show them a higher, more abundant life in Christ than what we were given. We want to pass along the best to our children and to their children. It's possible. You can overcome any limitations and overcome any negativity.

Psalm 78:41 says, "Yes, again and again they tempted God, And limited the Holy One of Israel." Israel grieved God because they limited Him. He was grieved when they said, "We can't do it. It will never happen. We can't have our own land. We will never be able to do it!" They limited God, and He was grieved.

You and I never want to grieve the Lord. Be the person who goes for God's best, the one who reaches for more. Be the one who may be too bold, but who is also the one out there, trusting God and saying, "Yes, Lord, I believe! I believe You when You say I can do it." Don't limit what God can do through you. Believe He has an abundant life—a promised land—an amazing destiny just for you!

Jesus has so much more abundant life planned for us. He has far more for us than we will ever believe. By renewing our minds to His Word, we begin to enter into His plan. Never let the condemnation of a religious world or the negativity or a sinful world hold you back. By the grace of God, you are His child. You have a wonderful destiny and eternity. This message of renewal and change should never be a pressure to perform or live up to. It is the grace of God that saves, heals, renews, and changes our lives. His grace makes us what we are; we are simply embracing His grace. We respond to Him, and He empowers us to become all He calls us to be.

The Bible teaches us that *by the grace of God, we are what we are*. His grace enables us to be changed into His image and fulfill His will. Let's believe the Lord's prayer is working every day, that *His will is done in us on Earth as it is in Heaven*. With God's grace and His help, I believe you will prosper in all things and be in health.

Your family will be blessed in every way. Your story will have an amazing end.

THIRTEEN

Detox Your Soul

From Casey and Wendy

It is our hearts' desire to inspire you and empower you to see real and lasting renewal in your life. By the grace of God, you can walk in new realms of life. To experience new things, we need new thoughts and new ways of thinking. With that in mind, we want to share a message from our oldest son Caleb in this last chapter. Caleb is like us in many ways. He is also seeking renewal and has brought new things to his family and ours. He has a wonderful way of seeing things from the Lord and presenting them to the Church. One of the most important things we must renew is how we see ourselves, the value and worth we put on ourselves. The following chapter with lift your self-esteem and help you see yourself through God's eyes.

Bonus Chapter from Caleb Treat

Detoxing is a big deal right now. When you go through a physical detox, it gets the junk out of your system and resets your body to function the way it should. Detoxing your body cleans it out and resets your eating habits—and the same is true with detoxing your soul. Detoxing your soul will let you remove the limitations that have been set in your life. As you reset the value you place on yourself, you also reset your limitations.

The limits of your life will be set by the value which you place on yourself. Your value—how you see yourself—is a huge part of how you live your life. You may not realize just how much of an effect your value—not your true value, but the value that you think you have—plays into your life.

If you see yourself as highly valuable, special, unique, and individual—you will have larger borders and fewer limits. But if you see yourself as not worth it—you devalue yourself, look down on yourself, are embarrassed about yourself, hesitant—you keep making your value lower and lower. Your world will keep shrinking. How you see your value establishes the limits on your life.

"Jesus said to him, 'You shall love the Lord your God with all your heart, with all your soul, with all your mind. This is the first and great commandment. And the second is like it: You shall love your neighbor as yourself. On these two commandments hang all the Law and the Prophets'" (Matthew 22:37-40).

You shall love your neighbor as you love yourself. This chapter goes on to say that on *these two concepts*—on these two principles—*"hang all the Law and the Prophets."* That means the entire Old Testament can be boiled down to this: *Love God and love people—as you love yourself.*

Most of us know these verses, but we usually remember them as loving God and loving people. What are the two great commandments? Love God and love people. We read, *love your neighbor*, and we stop right there. But it's not finished there. It's not done yet. The scripture goes on to say, *as you love yourself.*

If you don't know how to love yourself, this whole principle breaks down. You can't begin to make this work if you don't know how to love yourself, because loving your neighbor hinges on your ability to love yourself. The way you see yourself and the value you place on yourself will define the limits to the love you have for humanity. You can't love this world if you can't love yourself.

How large is your world? How big are your limits? Have you maxed out? Are you done with all your goals and desires? Do you have limits to your dreams, vision, and hope for a great future? Or will you stretch yourself and say, "God, what is it that You have for me? Like Paul said, I'm going to run my race. I'm going to finish it. I know You have more for me." Or do you think, *You don't know who I am. You don't know my past. No one has ever loved me. God can't use me*. You beat yourself down, and in the process you limit your life. In essence, you're limiting God by believing He can't use you. You don't know how to love yourself because your value is so low. You feel so broken, and you believe He can't use you.

The value that you set on something defines the way you treat it. If you value something highly, you'll treat it well. If you place a low value on it, you won't treat it well. Here's the perfect example. When you bought that brand-new car, you said something like, "No one's eating in the car! We're not doing the drive-through in this car! Nono-no, we aren't even folding the bag up tight, just until we get it home! I do not want that smell in my new car!" But, if you don't care about your car, it's a rental or just old, you'll take that thing off-roading. You'll even *make* the burgers in the car. You don't care. It doesn't matter because of the value you place on it. A brand-new car—*no food*. Rental car—*who cares?* It's all about value.

You have that nice outfit on because it's date-night with your wife. You're about to go out the door when your wife hands you the baby. You think, *Whoa, what? I just put my nice shirt on.* You value the clothes you are wearing, right? You don't want to hold the baby, because too much can happen in a second with a baby. You never know what's coming. Neither does the baby—there's just no warning. Suddenly you've got this spot on your good shirt. Value. You value the shirt. Now when you put on the old T-shirt, it doesn't even matter. You're wiping the stuff off the baby with your shirt! You think, *Let me get that.* But Sunday morning, I've got my suit on and I'm saying, "Don't hand me the baby right now. I'm going to church." Value.

Cost is often connected to value, but it's not the same thing. The price you pay for something is not its value. As an example, let's take a pair of jeans that cost $50. A high school kid, working a part-time job on the weekends, has to save for weeks and weeks before he can get those jeans. Once he does, he is going to value that pair of jeans because it took weeks to earn the money to buy them. But, let's say a few years later, the same person with a full-time job, making good money, is going to pick up a $50 pair of jeans like it's nothing. The price didn't change, but the value he placed on them did, and the way he treats those jeans will also dramatically change. The price did not define the value. The way he valued the jeans defined how he treated them. How you value something determines how you treat it.

How do you value yourself? How you value yourself sets the tone for how you'll treat yourself. If you value yourself, you won't talk down to yourself all the time. You won't think, *I'm such a loser. I can't believe I did that.* If you value your wife, you'll talk to her with respect. How do you treat the people in your world? How do you treat your friends, your boss, your co-workers? Do you value that collector's car more than you value the people in your life? You treat that one car in your garage really well. Your marriage would look really good if you treated your wife the same way. Value is communicated in your actions. Value defines how you treat someone—even yourself. What you value, you will treat well.

The world has an interesting value system. The government has set the *value of life* in multiple different ways. The Environmental Protection Agency sets the value of a human life at $9.1 million. The Food and Drug Administration sets the value of life at $7.9 million. The Department of Transportation sets the value of life at $6 million. But most private and government-run health insurance companies set the value of life at $50,000. A Stanford economist came up with the average value of a person for a year at somewhere around $129,000. Everyone is coming up with numbers on the monetary value of a human life.

If someone passes away in an accident, the family wants a *number* that represents the value of that person. If your spouse passes away in an accident and you blame someone, or you have life insurance, you expect some kind of payment for that life. You either have a predetermined amount of insurance, or you try to define a number that places a value on that person. The insurance company determines the monetary value based on whether they were old or young, whether they had a good job or not, and if they were healthy or not. All of a sudden they're trying to find a way to put a dollar value on the life of that person.

Most of us would never say this out loud, but we internally have a thought about how much we think we matter. Think about it like this: If I stood you up next to someone else—although you would never say it—you would have an opinion about whether you were more or less valuable than that person. We would never want anyone to be able to read our minds at that moment, but all of us do it. Because of our flesh—our human nature—we see someone else and think, *Yeah, I'm more (or less) valuable than that person*. We compare our value to theirs. If we're going to set our value, why don't we pursue the way God wants us to define it? We're constantly setting values on both ourselves and the people around us, so why not let God set our value?

Renewing the Mind 2.0

Does your net worth set your value? You have assets—a nice house and an expensive car, investments and properties, some stocks and bonds—and after you take away all the liabilities, you think, *I'm really doing well for myself.* That is your net worth. You think, *That's my value right there because, you know, I have a really high net worth.* Or maybe you care more about social things? Cultural things? Maybe you set your value on *Instagram likes?* You think, *People are liking me today! I got thirty likes!* Then the next day you get eleven likes, and you feel bad! You start thinking, *No one likes me! I only got eleven likes.*

How many of us set a value on ourselves because of social media? Does how many people "like" your *Instagram* post define how you feel? Wow, are you really letting that define the value you place on your life? Since the value you place on your life is defining the limits of your life, that means *Instagram* is now setting the limits of your life. I wouldn't say that's really true, but you are letting it define how you feel about yourself, and how you feel about yourself is defining how you see your value. Your value sets the limits of your life. In reality, *Instagram* has influence on the limitations you've allowed in your life.

No one follows me on Twitter. No one cares what I have to say. I need to get more friends on Facebook. I poked 38 people today, and nobody poked me back. Does poking still exist on *Facebook?* Here's the thing that hurts us—*cultural things change.* They're not true. They are just a trend. If you are setting your value on something that is a trend— and not truth—your value will never be true.

Instagram will go away one day. If you have set your value on something that won't exist someday, how do you really know your value? Let's go back a few years. How many remember when *MySpace* existed? Do you remember how important the "Top 8" was? That was a big deal. You would go to someone's page, and there were eight pictures and, in essence, those were their eight closest friends. Let's be honest. How many of you went to one of your friend's pages—and even though they were in your Top 8— you realized you weren't in their Top 8? And you thought, *Oh no, they didn't! They're not in my Top 8 anymore! I don't even care who I put in; it's just not going to be them.* You put your mom in your Top 8 because *they are out!* Suddenly, at that moment, you felt devalued because of *MySpace*. Today the Top 8 doesn't even exist. At the time, it felt so important, but you were setting your value on something that wasn't even true.

Cultural things aren't truth—they're just cultural. Years ago, when Jesus was here, men had long hair and wore dresses. That was cultural. That was the way it was done. Today, only long hair still exists! Jesus did it. I'm doing it! You see, it wasn't true or not—it was just cultural. It was accepted. It was a trend. How many people today set their value on whether or not they fit into the trend? You are setting your value on a trend or a look that will change. It has no lasting impact on your real value.

Why would we allow a trend to set the limits in our lives? How far can God take you if He doesn't know when you're just going to give up because the trend changes? *I don't know, God, You're really using me, but now bell bottoms are back in, and I just can't wear bell bottoms!* Wait a moment and our culture changes. Looks change, trends change, and you have lost your self-esteem? You saw yourself the wrong way.

You have to know the identity of something to set a correct value on it. When I was little, I had a signed baseball—a Ken Griffey Jr. How cool is that? One day my sister found it, and bless her heart, she wanted to help me by cleaning it. She thought it was just a dirty baseball—and who wants a dirty baseball, right? So she's thinking, *Let's clean this.* She got the dish soap and scrubbed it. It was squeaky clean. She thought, *Let's make this the best, cleanest baseball that's ever existed.* Because she didn't know the identity of the baseball, she couldn't value it correctly. You see, if you don't know the identity of something, you don't understand its value.

Recently I saw a story in the news about a man who is a car collector. He buys and sells old, classic cars. One day he saw an old, rusty, beat-up car in a barn and asked the owner, "How much for that car?"

The man said, "Well, it doesn't work right now—hasn't run for years. $1,800 and it's yours."

The man said, "Done! I'll take that car." Today, that car is going to auction, and it is estimated to sell for $150,000-$180,000! A previously restored version of that same car sold for $900,000!

The seller didn't know its identity, so he lost out on a lot of money. If you don't know the identity of something, you'll never understand its value. When the buyer saw it, he would have paid a lot more for it because he knew there was still a profit to be had! But the owner didn't know it's value—didn't know how to identify it—and sold it for so much less than what it was worth.

How many of us are underselling ourselves because we don't know our identity? How many live lives that undersell the destiny God wrote when He created them? Are you underselling yourself and the plans and purposes God has for you? If you don't know your identity—don't know who you are—then you can't define your value. If you can't define your value, you truly don't know the limits of your life.

John 1:1-3 really helps us define our identity: "In the beginning was the Word, and the Word was with God, and the Word was God. He was in the beginning with God. All things were made through Him, and without Him nothing was made that was made."

John is opening his gospel by talking about Jesus, showing who Jesus is. When this was originally written in the Greek, there were two words commonly used to define our English word, *Word*. They are *logos* and *rhema*. You may have heard of these words, but I want to show how they both apply to this passage, which will then define who you are.

Logos refers to the entirety of a message. *Rhema* is defined as a specific word that is spoken or revealed from *logos*. In essence, the entire Bible is *logos* and *rhema*. The whole Bible is *logos*, but a verse of the Bible would be *rhema*. *Logos* is an idea or concept, and when it is spoken, it becomes *rhema*. So the spoken word is a *rhema* expression of the *logos* word.

Logos also is defined as a concept of deity. *Logos* is a whole message, a word and a concept of deity. *Rhema* is the spoken *logos*, an individual message, a life-form of the *logos*. So you have *logos*, and then a small part turns into *rhema*. Both are referring to—Word.

Let's read the same verses in John, chapter one, and insert the Greek word *logos* to see how *the Word* is being communicated: In the beginning was the Word, which is *Logos* or Jesus, and the *Logos* was with God, and the *Logos* was God. He, the *Logos*, was in the beginning with God. All things were made through Him, the *Logos*, and without *Logos* nothing was made that was made. In the beginning was this concept of deity, and this concept took life and became Jesus; but before He took life in human form, He made all of creation.

Logos is an idea or a concept, and when it's spoken, when it's revealed, a small expression of the large concept turns into *rhema*.

In the beginning, nothing was created without *Logos,* and through *Logos* all was created. So Jesus is Logos and spoke you into creation. You're His creation. He made you. So literally, there is *Logos*, and then there's you. You're the *rhema* expression of the concept of Jesus. He spoke you into creation. In the beginning was all this, and God spoke creation into being. You're literally the *rhema* expression of Jesus.

When you start realizing that your identity is founded on the revelation of Jesus, your value must be reset. When who you are is a literal expression of Jesus, you are created through the concept of deity. *Rhema* took life, and you're here! That just blows my mind! Before, it was all just a concept, and that concept gave life, gave birth, and it became *rhema*, and it began to dwell on this Earth. And that's you!

When you begin to realize that your identity is based in Jesus, your values have to become realigned. You have to shift it all up and think, *Wait a minute! I'm not devaluing myself anymore.* Your value is not set by the parent who spoke down to you. Your value is not set by that boyfriend who left you. Your value is not set by that divorce. Your value is not set by that addiction you had to overcome. Your value is not set by your past. Your value is set by your identity, and your identity is Jesus.

When you look at the old car, that owner missed the *identity* of it. Once the car was identified, the value took life. Once you're identified, your value is given. Your identity is Jesus. Your identity.

Let that get into your soul today. Your identity. Who you are is like Jesus—a son or daughter of God, a child of God.

I would assume that the princes of the Royal British family have never felt bad about living in the palace. I doubt there was ever a moment when they said, "Are you sure I can live here? Are you sure it is okay for me to sleep in this bed? Should I be in here?" No. Why? Because they know who they are. They fully believe, *This is my house.* Well it's not theirs yet, it's actually the queen's, but their attitude is, *It's mine. I'm only a child, but I know it's mine!*

My daughter, Willow, has not once been hesitant to receive something from me. I've never heard her say, "Are you sure, Dad? It seems like a lot." No, she's ready to receive everything I give her. We got into a little bit of a bad habit, where I would come home from work, and she'd say, "Surprise?"

Sometimes I would have to say, "I don't have anything for you today, Willow."

She would say, "Oh, okay." Immediately I would think, *I'll go get something. I'll be right back.*

My wife Christa would say, "Don't leave! You may not buy her another prize right now!"

Why does Willow have that attitude? Because she knows who she is. She's my daughter. She belongs in our house. She knows we give her nice things and take care of her because she knows her identity. Have you ever seen a child start crying because you're holding someone else's kid? You know what I'm talking about? It's like a little bit of rivalry or something. Willow will say, "No, that's *my* dad. *My* dad only gets to hold *me*." Why? Because she knows her identity.

As Christians, we need to have a bit more faith to look at God and say, "I'm Your daughter! I'm Your son! This is my home. This is my place. I belong in the realm of favor. I belong in the realm of grace. It is mine because I am Yours." When you know your identity, it affects how you act.

What's your value today? Remember, I started by writing that *price doesn't define value*. But many times, price has a way of setting a value. I'll give you an example. When you sell your house, you don't set the value by how much lumber it took to build it. You set the price based on what people are willing to pay in the current market. That price is always shifting, but the market sets the value of your house. So the price is not set by the average price; it's set by the highest price. The highest price someone is willing to pay for your house sets the value of what you will sell it for. The highest price.

Willow loves Beanie Babies. She actually loves Beanie Babies without the tag because she pulls them all off. Let's say a Beanie Baby costs one dollar to manufacture. With the material and other costs, someone spent a dollar to make one Beanie Baby. Then they sold it to a distributor, and that distributor paid two dollars for the Beanie Baby. The distributor sold it to a store, and that store bought it for say, six dollars. You then bought it at the store for twelve dollars.

At the beginning of the chain, that Beanie Baby was only valued at one dollar; but by the time you got it, it was valued at twelve dollars. You have to pay the highest price set. You can't buy straight from the manufacturer or from the distributor. You have to buy from the store. The store set the value at twelve dollars, so if you want the Beanie Baby, you have to pay its value. And its value keeps changing.

There are a few Beanie Babies that have amazing value. Right now, on *Ebay*, you can pay $652,000 for a Beanie Baby! That is nuts. So how much would you have to pay for *that* Beanie Baby? You would have to pay its value—and someone said that its value is $652,000.

And they'll even throw in free shipping!

So although that Beanie Baby has a value set at $652,000 dollars, it only took one dollar to make. The distributor paid two dollars to purchase it. A store probably sold it for around twelve dollars. Now someone wants to sell that Beanie Baby for $652,000. So what is the value of the Beanie Baby? Is it one dollar, two dollars, twelve dollars—or is it, $652,000? It's $652,000. Why? Because the value is placed at the highest price someone was willing to pay.

What is the highest price someone's been willing to pay for you? That is what should define your value. If you're unsure of that answer, the answer is *Jesus*. Jesus was willing to give His life for you. So the highest price that was paid for you was the life of Jesus. When someone asks you, "What are you valued at?" the answer is Jesus, because the highest price has been set.

No longer are you valued as a *one-night stand*. No longer are you valued as someone *to walk over*. No longer are you valued as *second best*. Others might not see your value, but that just means they don't get you. That means they're not going to be a part of your life. It doesn't mean that you have to reset your value to what they see. Your value has already been set.

Why would a person sell that Beanie Baby for a hundred dollars when someone set its value at $652,000? God has already set your value, so stop underselling yourself! Those old friends who won't let you change—they can't see your true value, so stop changing to fit in with their values. Don't allow them to pull you down and redefine your value, when Jesus has already set your value.

Where is your value today? Here's how I see it: Your value sets the limits to your life. When you begin to see both your identity and value—who you are and the price that Jesus was willing to pay—no longer should you accept the world's limits. You should be limitless. No longer should you have low expectations and a ceiling on your future. You should have no limits, because Jesus set your value at His life.

What can't you do? Where can't you go? What business can't you start? You can do all things through Christ who strengthens you (Philippians 4:13). You can have a phenomenal marriage, because you're valued at that level. You can be limitless because your value is priceless. Take the borders off your life. Begin to dream in ways only God can fulfill. When we say at church, "Be You," that's what we mean. Be you. You know who you are. You are the expression of Jesus in this world. Stop trying to live up to someone else. Stop trying to be someone else, and *be you*. You are a unique, original expression of our Creator. Be you.

How to Be Born Again

Every person on Earth has sinned and is in need of a personal relationship with God. Romans 3:23 says, **"All have sinned and fall short of the glory of God."**

To have a personal relationship with God, you must believe in the Lord Jesus Christ as your Lord and Savior. According to John 3:16, it is through believing in Jesus that we receive eternal life: **"For God so loved the world that He gave His only begotten Son, that whoever believes in Him should not perish but have everlasting life."**

When you are born again, you can know God and have everlasting life. John 3:3 says, **"Jesus answered and said to him, 'Most assuredly, I say to you, unless one is born again, he cannot see the kingdom of God.'"**

Being born again is the gift of God. It cannot be earned, and you cannot achieve it on your own. Romans 6:23 says, **"For the wages of sin is death, but the gift of God is eternal life in Christ Jesus our Lord."**

Ephesians 2:8-9 makes it clear: **"For it is by grace you have been saved, through faith—and this not from yourselves, it is the gift of God—not by works, so that no one can boast."**

When you are born again, you receive Jesus as your Lord and Master, and you commit yourself to follow His Word (the Bible). Romans 10:9-10 says, **"That if you confess with your mouth the Lord Jesus and believe in your heart that God has raised Him from the dead, you will be saved. For with the heart one believes unto righteousness, and with the mouth confession is made unto salvation."**

First John 2:3 tells us it is a commitment: **"Now by this we know that we know Him, if we keep His commandments."**

If you are ready to make this life-changing commitment, then pray according to Romans 10:9-10:

God, I come to You in the Name of Jesus. I ask You to come into my life. I confess with my mouth that Jesus is my Lord, and I believe in my heart that You have raised Him from the dead. I turn my back on sin, and I commit to follow You for the rest of my life. I thank You, Father, for saving me!

Welcome to the family of Christ! You are now born again, forgiven, and on your way to Heaven. You are a new creation in Christ Jesus. Second Corinthians 5:17 says, **"Therefore, if anyone is in Christ, he is a new creation; old things have passed away; behold, all things have become new."**

Yet this is only the beginning of your new life as a Christian. As you study God's Word and apply its truths to your life, you will renew your mind and grow as a Christian.

Romans 12:1-2 says, **"I beseech you therefore, brethren, by the mercies of God, that you present your bodies a living sacrifice, holy, acceptable to God, which is your reasonable service. And do not be conformed to this world, but be transformed by the renewing of your mind, that you may prove what is that good and acceptable and perfect will of God."**

Become a part of a church where the Word of God is preached in truth and you can be encouraged by other believers. Hebrews 10:25 says, **"...not forsaking the assembling of ourselves together, as is the manner of some, but exhorting one another, and so much the more as you see the Day approaching."**

If doubts or fears come to your mind that you are not truly born again, reject them and realize that God's Word is what your salvation is based on not what you think or feel.

Romans 10:9-10, the verses you based your prayer on, say, **"That if you confess with your mouth the Lord Jesus and believe in your heart that God has raised Him from the dead, you will be saved. For with the heart one believes unto righteousness, and with the mouth confession is made unto salvation."**

Part of the Christian walk is to publicly acknowledge your decision through being baptized in water. John the Baptist baptized Jesus in the Jordan River. Jesus desires that those who accept Him be baptized also. Acts 10:48 says, **"And he commanded them to be baptized in the name of the Lord."**

To help you succeed on this Earth as a Christian, God has also given you the gift of the Holy Spirit. He is your helper.

Being Filled With the Holy Spirit

The Holy Spirit is your comforter and teacher. He has been given to you to help you in your everyday life. John 14:26 says, **"But the Helper, the Holy Spirit, whom the Father will send in My name, He will teach you all things, and bring to your remembrance all things that I said to you."**

The Holy Spirit will give you the power to be a strong witness for Jesus. Acts 1:8 says, **"But you shall receive power when the Holy Spirit has come upon you; and you shall be witnesses to Me in Jerusalem, and in all Judea and Samaria, and to the end of the earth."**

When you are filled with the Holy Spirit, you can speak in other tongues for the purpose of prayer, prophesying, worship, and personal edification. Acts 2:4 says, **"And they were all filled with the Holy Spirit and began to speak with other tongues, as the Spirit gave them utterance."**

The Holy Spirit is for every born again person. You don't have to wait or work to receive Him. Acts 2:38-39 tells us, **"Then Peter said to them, 'Repent, and let every one of you be baptized in the name of Jesus Christ for the remission of sins; and you shall receive the gift of the Holy Spirit. For the promise is to you and to your children, and to all who are afar off, as many as the Lord our God will call.'"**

When you receive the Holy Spirit and speak in other tongues, your mind will not understand anything you are saying. It will sound useless and foolish to you, but you are speaking mysteries to God not to yourself or to other people.

First Corinthians 14:2 says, **"For he who speaks in a tongue does not speak to men but to God, for no one understands him; however, in the spirit he speaks mysteries."**

Speaking in tongues is an act of your will. God gives you the ability to do it, but He will not force you or do it for you. First Corinthians 14:1415 says, **"For if I pray in a tongue, my spirit prays, but my understanding is unfruitful. What is the conclusion then? I will pray with the spirit, and I will also pray with the understanding. I will sing with the spirit, and I will also sing with the understanding."**

If you ask for the Holy Spirit in faith, God the Father will give Him to you: **"If you then, being evil, know how to give good gifts to** your children, how much more will your heavenly Father give the Holy Spirit to those who ask Him!" (Luke 11:13).

Would you like to receive the Holy Spirit today?

If so, pray according to Luke 11:13, asking God to fill you with the Holy Spirit:

Father, I come to You in the Name of Jesus. I ask You to fill me with Your Holy Spirit. I receive Him from You and according to the Bible I will now pray in other tongues as the Spirit gives me the utterance. Thank You, Father!

After praying this prayer asking God to fill you, pray confidently in other tongues. As you pray regularly in other tongues, it will build you up and charge up your spirit man. Jude 1:20 says, **"But you, beloved, building yourselves up on your most holy faith, praying in the Holy Spirit."**

How to Recommit Your Life to Christ

If you have made Jesus the Lord of your life but have fallen away from living a Christian life, you can recommit your life to God.

Simply confess and admit your sin to Him. He is faithful to forgive.

First John 1:9 says, **"If we confess our sins, He is faithful and just to forgive us our sins and to cleanse us from all unrighteousness."**

Once you confess your sins and receive God's forgiveness, thank Him for forgiving you. He is a just and loving God.

Next, seek out a Bible-believing and Bible-teaching church. You need to be trained in the Word of God so you can grow in your Christian walk.

—Casey and Wendy Treat

About the Authors

In January 1980, with a group of thirty people, Pastors Casey and Wendy Treat started Christian Faith Center in Seattle, Washington. Christian Faith Center is a multi-cultural, multi-campus church in the Pacific Northwest. In addition to serving thousands of people through weekly church services, countless others are inspired through the Treat's global media outreach, *Casey Treat Ministries*, and television broadcast, *Successful Living with Casey Treat*.

As a teenager, Casey was involved with drugs and a worldly lifestyle. In 1974, at the age of nineteen, he entered a drug rehabilitation program. During his years there, he was born again and learned how to renew his mind through the Word of God. Casey and Wendy met at Seattle Bible College where he received a Bachelor in Theology degree.

In 2009 and 2010 respectively, Casey Treat and Wendy Treat received Honorary Doctorate in Theology degrees from Hansei University in Seoul, South Korea (Dr. David Yonggi Cho & Dr. Kim Sunghae Cho), recognizing their accomplishments in ministry.

Traveling extensively each year, Casey and Wendy speak globally at conventions and churches. Their books, CD's/DVD's and podcasts are distributed worldwide.

The Treats have been married for over 38 years and have three grown children.

Requests for information should be directed to:

Casey Treat Ministries
PO Box 98800
Seattle, WA 98198
1-253-943-2400
www.caseytreat.com

Follow Pastors Casey and Wendy on social media:

Facebook: Casey Treat/Wendy Treat
Twitter: @caseytreat @wendytreat
Instagram: @caseydtreat @wendytreat

Other Teaching Materials by Casey and Wendy Treat available at www.caseytreat.com.

Printed in Great Britain
by Amazon